HOW TO CREATE A TREASURE LEGACY COLLECTION:

The Ultimate Guide to Living Your Best Life Now

How to Create a Treasure Legacy Collection

For more information, email Hello@EarthAdventuresForKids.com

ISBN: 979-8-89109-417-8 - paperback

ISBN: 979-8-89109-418-5 - ebook

Dedicated to all the parents, guardians, grandparents, caregivers, and mentors who stay up late, get up early, research, look for, find, keep, toss, improve, let go, and do all the things that go into caregiving and raising happy, healthy kids into happy, healthy adulthood—also including caregivers who care for adults and elderly parents. May you find what you need when you need it and celebrate all your wins.

The Earth Adventures For Kids

Signature Collection and Treasure Legacy Collection

are not just for parents and grandparents!

★ We believe everyone is a kid at heart, regardless of age. Earth Adventures For Kids is for everyone, from age zero to one hundred and beyond—anyone can benefit from the Mindset, Tools, Systems, and Marketplace.

★ Share our books with mentors, counselors, teachers, coaches, friends, family, caregivers of all kinds, and community members; everyone benefits.

OUR TLC METHOD HAS LED TO GREAT RESULTS.

Read our reviews . . .

"The Wondering Mat creates a space and place to remind us as parents to slow down and take care of ourselves mentally, physically, spiritually, and emotionally. Our teenagers are drawn to it, too! The demands of family life quiet down as we take our practice of renewing and calming on The Wondering Mat. Looking forward to adding in more Earth Adventures For Kids products and tools."

A. Edmonds, mom of two busy teenagers, doctor's wife, and household manager with a degree in Economics from UC Davis

"The book *How to Create a Financial Worksheet* and all the tools in it have helped me with my financial organization, home and office organization, and legacy. The Financial Worksheet helped me "find money" and re-structure a few things, *allowing me to buy a new car!* My mode of operation around the house is better for me and my family. I am now better at being the mom and grandma I want to be."

P. Nettles, mom of five and grandma extraordinaire, tax and administrative professional for over thirty years

"My mom completed the 90-day Coaching Programs for the Financial Worksheet and the Treasure Legacy Collection. In 2021, she went into the hospital with coronavirus. I stepped in and helped with her finances; it was so easy to do because she completed her coaching with Earth Adventures For Kids. Having her TLC done helped me and my family in many ways. I recommend that every parent and grandparent read these books and take action."

M. Flynn, foster mom of teenager, former middle school English teacher, realtor

TABLE OF CONTENTS

INTRODUCTION TO THE BASICS
OF EARTH ADVENTURES FOR KIDS . . .

Find out why our books are the ultimate guides
to improving your life and legacy and living your best life now!

Our TLC Method helps you:

★ Achieve synergy and harmony in your household.

★ Celebrate and extract richness from meaningful experiences and milestones in life.

★ Set new goals and a vision for your future.

★ Reset, renew, and calm anxiety.

★ Identify what is working and what is not working.

★ Decide what needs to change.

★ Improve your decision-making.

★ Master the art of organizing.

Connect the dots to see better outcomes and results when you and your household members practice positive habits and routines in organized spaces of your home, office, and finances.

Unlock the power of organization with our books, tools, and systems that also captivate the imagination. Creating a comprehensive overall picture, see how our TLC Method works to help you accomplish your goals, vision, and mission for your household.

When everything falls apart and things don't go as planned, our TLC Method—with books, tools, and systems—helps get you and your household members back on a positive trajectory. Navigating through turmoil and unplanned events is a skill that can be improved. You can chart the course from point A to B and lead your family to places you want to be. Often, as parents, we felt like we were "herding cats" who would not follow and just did their own thing. At times, it seemed we could not accomplish goals in a joyful, respectful way in harmony with the entire household membership. This is where the term "get with the program" came from, and we needed everyone to "get with the program."

Who decides what "the program" is anyway? Is it you as a parent and caregiver? Our books and tools help you develop your "program" and show everyone their part to play. Every household member can familiarize themselves with our TLC Method to create household systems that facilitate everyone reaching goals and completing daily tasks and objectives in a way that improves relationships and communication while building a positive, long-lasting legacy.

TLC is an acronym for "tender, loving, care" and "Treasure Legacy Collection." The TLC Method is about using our books and tools to send your tender, loving, care "TLC" with our

Treasure Legacy Collection "TLC." In the process, get organized, improve communication, and build your legacy daily as a way of life.

Bring household members into solutions with our TLC Method. Have regular meetings and share stories of how our books and tools helped you in your days and nights. You will always think of new ways to apply our books and tools to improve your days and nights. The possibilities are endless. Organization, function, efficiency, joy, humor, and peace of mind all come into play in this entire "program" of life.

Celebrate achievements and celebrate times when each person uses our books and tools to make a situation better. Recognize and acknowledge each other when you see positive changes in habits, practices, and routines, and then connect the actions to match with the improved results and outcomes.

OUR BOOKS AND TOOLS ARE TIMELESS.

As time passes and phases of life evolve, our books and tools will mean different things to different people at different levels. Discuss this. For example, we discovered that the book *How to Create a Treasure Legacy Collection: The Ultimate Guide to Living Your Best Life Now* could be used when our children were small, but as they grew into adulthood, we realized they could use the book as young adults. In addition, we now use the book with our aging parents. There are infinite ways to use our books and tools, and we look forward to hearing your success stories.

We like to look back in life and see when we started using the tools and how we have used them over time. We see new applications for our books and tools for our future lives, and the 5 TLC Legacy Lists we create with our books are a foundation for our intentional living.

Consider your quality of life, relationships, and whether or not you are moving forward in the direction you want to go. Is there alignment in values and goals in your household? Is there support and synergy?

Distractions, competing interests, limiting beliefs, poor nutrition, disorganization, lack of exercise, and insufficient self-care keep us from accomplishing our goals and fulfilling our life vision. Our books and tools help you with decision-making skills, priorities, defining values, and developing the right mindset so that, come what may, you have what it takes to succeed.

Which best describes your household vibes in the past?

happy, humorous, gracious, forgiving, appreciative, cooperative, optimistic or

argumentative, complaint-filled, judgmental, stubborn, problematic

What would you like more of in the future?

Our TLC Method can help.

At the heart of Earth Adventures For Kids is the relationship of **Mindset, Tools, Systems, and Marketplace**. Heart and mind take time and place to receive inspiration, vision, awareness, purpose, creativity, goals, and aspirations. This process and experience of what some may call "divine revelation" is unique to each person and each phase of life.

A pillar of both our Signature Collection and Treasure Legacy Collection is **The Wondering Mat.** As you read our books, you will learn more about why it is a pillar. It was named The Wondering Mat for many reasons. One reason is inspired by the following definition of the word "wondering" by John English. He was asked on Quora.com, "What is the difference between wondering and thinking?" He explained, "Both are a mental process. Thinking is the more rational action, one that includes analysis, planning, and other processes. Wondering is a cross between curiosity and savoring the amazing aspects of life and the physical realities we interact with." He posted a beautiful picture of a rainbow, and he then stated that thinking about the rainbow is worthwhile, but it is better to view it as an "object of wonder."

HOW TO LIVE YOUR BEST LIFE.

Mindset is listed first in our Mindset, Tools, Systems, and Marketplace sequence because it deals with the concept of our thinking being first in creating our lifestyle. *As a Man Thinketh* is a book written in 1902 by James Allen. (Gender note: Man refers to all humans and our shared human experience). "This book explains and promotes **the direct connection between our thoughts and our happiness.** It emphasizes the **importance of positive thinking and the power of belief in bringing about positive events in one's life.** In the book, Allen argues that '. . . each man holds the key to every condition, good or bad, that enters into his life, and that, by working patiently and intelligently upon his thoughts, he may remake his life and transform his circumstances.'"

This concept is also shown in Romans 12:2 KJV where Paul the writer tells us to **be transformed by the renewing of our minds.** Faith Chapel, located in northern California, states on their website the following explanation of Romans 12:2, "Meaning: Are you living your best life? Shifting your patterns and focus can change your life. That's what this verse is about—renewing your mind, changing the way you think to create a better life for yourself. . . ." https://agfaithchapel.org

Mentors of the Earth Adventures For Kids team and many other "successful" people teach the concept of using a positive mindset when setting and reaching goals. We placed the word successful in quotations because every person has a unique definition of success, and we help you define yours.

"BOOKS CHANGE LIVES."

This quote is from publisher Chandler Bolt. We agree and we always say, "Read our books," because our books are our way of communicating with you one-to-one on how we became wildly successful according to our definition of success. Our books will help you define your terms of success and understand the mindset, tools, systems, and marketplace that are key to living your best life. So, read our books!

Taking time to let your mind ponder and wander with purpose and intention yields great results! With the constructive focus of renewal, reset, reprogramming, and calm, one can seek and find solutions to problems and gain vision for the day, week, month, season, and year. This positive time-out inspires creativity and builds inner fortitude and strength while getting the resolution to succeed.

Taking time to let the mind ponder and wander with purpose and intention allows time to identify and release anxiety, fear, worry, and harmful thought patterns. This time allows a process of transformation into what you do want, such as taking time to make "I am" statements like "I am strong," "I am wealthy," and "I am healthy."

Taking time to receive inspiration on The Wondering Mat can help you see the next steps on your roadmap to attaining your goals with your aligned values—helping you rise up to live the life you want. The subconscious mind materializes what your beliefs and thoughts tell it. For more on this, search online for "the power of thoughts and beliefs to get desired results." Sometimes, life pulls at us in all directions, and we get scattered to the point of being ineffective, which can hinder our desired results from manifesting.

Taking time to renew and reset on The Wondering Mat
allows your brain to defragment and your nervous system to calm
so you can see the most effective next steps that will lead you to the results you want.

Taking time to let the mind be infused with positivity, direction, guidance, and inspiration is powerful, especially if we use our mat time to listen to mentors who are currently in the stages of success we aspire to reach. We can learn from those who have walked the walk and join their networks of people with similar goals and values. We can also look to see whom we can mentor and who may need our expertise in an area of life. Often, we get inspired when we can help others learn through our experiences. We mentor others as we are mentored!

On The Wondering Mat, watch for those unwanted thoughts that may creep in and go on a repeat loop. Learn how to "take unwanted thoughts captive" and release them powerfully. Replace negative and unproductive thoughts with a calm sense of confidence, purpose, and a clear vision of goals. Sometimes, it takes several days or even a week of prayer and processing to get the breakthrough, depending upon the circumstances at hand. If settling your mind is a struggle, various activities can help, such as vigorous exercise, listening to motivational music, time in nature, lifting weights, and cold-water therapy like a cold shower. These activities help break the repeat loop of unwanted thoughts.

Do some online research on the benefits of taking time to ponder. From the "12 Secret Benefits of Doing Nothing" online article by Radiant Life Chiropractic, ". . . 'Best Life' points out that in our turbulent and complex times, we could all benefit from a little unstructured time to regroup. Our lives are so busy, between work, family responsibilities, and social obligations, with every available scrap of free time eaten up by social media, round-the-clock news coverage, email, and hobbies. It's hard to squeeze in any time at all that isn't programmed for maximum productivity, yet it turns out there are significant advantages to doing absolutely nothing." https://getradiantlife.com/12-secret-benefits-of-doing-nothing/

Do some online research on the benefits of taking time to let your mind wander. In the American Psychological Association online article, "Put Down Devices, Let Your Mind Wander, Study Suggests," we learn "'Humans have a striking ability to immerse themselves in their own thinking,' said study lead author Aya Hatano, Ph.D., of Kyoto University in Japan. Our research suggests that individuals have difficulty appreciating just how engaging thinking can be. That could explain why people prefer keeping themselves busy with devices and other distractions rather than taking a moment for reflection and imagination in daily life." https://www.apa.org/news/press/releases/2022/07/thoughts-mind-wander

Later in the article, the study co-author, Kou Murayama, says, "That missed opportunity comes at a cost because previous studies have shown that spending time letting your mind wander has some benefits, according to the researchers. It can help people solve problems, enhance their creativity, and even help them find meaning in life. 'By actively avoiding thinking activities, people may miss these important benefits.'"

I have a t-shirt that says, "Hold on let me overthink this." When I wear it, I get so many comments from people telling me that they overthink too. So, as with much in life, we need to balance. I learned in my 20s that I need to balance my thinking time with my activity time which does not require so much thinking.

OUR "INNER LIFE" WORK IMPROVES OUR "OUTER LIFE" WORK.

I started taking step aerobics classes at our local gym and I enjoyed the upbeat music and the call-and-response format in which we went into "auto-pilot" listening to the cues from the fitness instructor. After months of getting good at responding to the fast-paced cues in my fitness classes, I noticed my college course grades improving, along with my ability to study, focus, and take tests. I attributed this to exercising different parts of my brain, making new connections, and sharpening my ability to focus.

The movie *Inside Out* by Disney demonstrates the meaning of "thinking straight" with their "train of thought" symbolized by an actual train in the movie. When we take time on The Wondering Mat, we can calm and focus, reset and renew, and think straight with a train of thought that leads us to great results, especially when prayer, thanksgiving, gratitude, and forgiveness to ourselves and others, are mixed in. *Inside Out* is a wonderful example of how thoughts, emotions, the brain, expectations, choices, and perspective all converge into our inner experiences, mental health, and overall well-being. This movie is great at giving visuals to an unseen world of inner life. It's still my husband's favorite movie! We watched it as a family when our daughter was in junior high, and it helped us all. You could watch this movie and see how all the elements of inner life work together. The Wondering Mat gives you a place to let this inner work happen.

Kids and adults have a lot in common!

I attended a lecture by Tina Payne Bryson, Ph.D. author of *The Whole-Brain Child,* and learned that **the techniques they use for kids can also be used with adults.** We can teach ourselves to identify what side of the brain we are using and then do activities that integrate the whole brain which yields beneficial results like experiencing calm and joy.

"In this pioneering, practical book, Daniel J. Siegel, neuropsychiatrist and author of the bestselling book Mindsight, and parenting expert Tina Payne Bryson demystify the meltdowns and aggravation, explaining the new science of how a child's brain is wired and how it matures. The "upstairs brain," which makes decisions and balances emotions, is under construction until the mid-twenties. And especially in young children, the right brain and its emotions tend to rule over the logic of the left brain. No wonder kids can seem-and feel-so out of control. By applying these discoveries to everyday parenting, you can turn any outburst, argument, or fear into a chance to integrate your child's brain and foster vital growth. Raise calmer, happier children using twelve key strategies. . . ." I read the book and I use the strategies as an adult—you can too!

At Earth Adventures For Kids, we say, **"Mindset, Tools, Systems, and Marketplace"** because, from **mindset**, we take action. **Tools** help us take action and be more effective. When we integrate tools into **systems**, they help us have positive disciplines, habits, and practices, and we can get better results. We learn when and where to use the tools and how to improve upon current tools and systems to propel us into a continual upward spiral of achieving results and accomplishing our goals and objectives. We gain confidence. We experience beneficial results, become resilient, and life becomes a fun obstacle course in which hurdles are handled with agility, skill, and know-how.

An interesting take on the obstacle course is parkour, which you have likely seen in videos, video games, and movies. "Parkour (French: [paʁkuʁ]) is an athletic training discipline or sport in which practitioners (called traceurs) attempt to get from point A to point B in the fastest and most efficient way possible. . . . With roots in military obstacle course training and martial arts, parkour includes running, climbing, swinging, vaulting, jumping, plyometrics, rolling, gymnastics, and quadrupedal movement—whatever is suitable for a given situation. . . . It involves seeing one's environment in a new way and envisioning the potential for navigating it by movement around, across, through, over, and under its features . . ." https://en.wikipedia.org/wiki/Parkour

We are not saying that we need to actually do acrobatics or become a "traceur in parkour" or do military courses, but we can **metaphorically look at life as an obstacle course** in which we have our positive discipline mindset, use tools, and develop systems to move through the days and nights and achieve our goals, with our "eyes on the prize." The prize for each of us will be different at different times.

Definition of Mindset: The Berkeley Well-being Institute defines mindset as follows, ". . . the set of attitudes or beliefs that we hold. Mindset is crucially important because our attitudes and beliefs affect everything we do, feel, think, and experience. Our mindset influences our perceptions and how we move through the world. Although we have one overall mindset, this can be made up of many smaller mindsets. Some of these help us improve our well-being and succeed in the world. Others hurt our ability to do so. That's why developing certain mindsets can greatly help us reach

our goals, enjoy our lives, and be more successful." https://www.berkeleywellbeing.com/mindsets.html

Reflection, attitude, perseverance, determination, creativity, imagination, beliefs, knowledge, desire, motivation, and more all converge into mindset. From this, we can take action and get the results we want.

Definition of Tool: Oxford Languages defines tools as follows, "A tool is an instrument that you use to help you accomplish some task." Earth Adventures For Kids has developed tools to help you define your values and what makes you "classic," helping you accomplish your goals.

Definition of Classic: Oxford Languages defines classic as follows, "Judged over a period of time to be of the highest quality and outstanding of its kind . . . a work of art of recognized and established value."

Definition of Systems: Oxford Languages defines a system as follows, "A set of things working together as parts of a mechanism or an interconnecting network . . . a set of principles or procedures according to which something is done; an organized framework or method."

Definition of Marketplace: Bluecart.com defines a marketplace as follows, "A marketplace is any location, whether in person or online, that facilitates the exchange of goods between buyers and sellers."

In The Marketplace, we have found many solutions to problems and challenges we have faced. We share The Marketplace with the Earth Adventures For Kids community to help each person seek and find solutions to their problems and continue adding these solutions as tools to their toolbox for success on the journey of life.

Get Familiar with the Tools and Create Your Own Systems.

Here are some examples of using the Earth Adventures For Kids
tools as a system in your days and nights:

- **Use our book** *101 Things to Do Other Than Social Media* as an idea generator on what activities to do over the weekends, holidays, rainy days, after school, and more.

- **Use the same book** as a checklist when creating your Treasure Legacy Collection. Keep notes of what you did, with whom, and when; these activities together can improve relationships and quality of life and the experiences become your stories. Place the stories into your TLC Journal/Binder or TLC Save Forever Box. You can do the activities solo as well, and we will discuss this later in the book.

- As part of your Treasure Legacy Collection, **use the same book** to create your Activities in My Name List, to create memories with loved ones now, and to instruct others how they can carry on in your name in the event of your absence. For those left behind, this list is comforting and bridges the gap between Heaven and Earth.

- Use Catch-All Bags and The Megaphone for the activities and outings you complete **with the same book**, and then keep treasures collected from these activities and events in your Save Forever Box to enjoy memories later.

Discover the many facets of the Earth Adventures For Kids Mindset, Tools, Systems, and Marketplace such as organization in the home and office, inspiration, communication, financial organization, legacy creation, definition of goals and values, super-nutrition, and optimization of energy which can all result in sleeping better, calming anxiety, and increasing energy. In turn, this allows refreshing, renewing, and joy to happen. All of the above can result in improved legacy, relationships, and quality of life.

Read our two foundational books, *How to Create Your Own Signature Collection* and *How to Create a Treasure Legacy Collection,* to learn our tools and systems. They are truly the ultimate guides in helping you improve your life and legacy and live your best life now.

Read our Journal Stories at www.EarthAdventuresForKids.com to learn how each tool came to be and how we used it with other tools to create an integrated system that still helps us through our days and nights in the form of home and office organization, legacy, finances, health, wealth, peace of mind, improved relationships, and quality of life.

To sum it all up, use the TLC Method for your roadmap to success.

THE COMPONENTS OF THE TLC METHOD ARE:

- ✓ **Mindset:** Getting your mindset aligned with your defined values and setting goals.

- ✓ **Tools:** Getting key tools for your toolbox to help you reach your goals.

- ✓ **Systems:** Integrating mindset and tools into your systems to achieve your goals.

- ✓ **Marketplace:** Using The Marketplace as a tool to find solutions to your problems and add these solutions as tools to your toolbox to help you be successful in life. It's a tool to find more tools!

We use the TLC Method of Mindset, Tools, Systems, and Marketplace and we have been wildly successful. We have developed our books and tools, including the TLC Method, to help get us where we want to be in life, and now we are sharing them with you.

Whatever the situation or space in life, learn to apply the TLC Method of Mindset, Tools, Systems, and Marketplace. We hope applying the TLC Method helps you, too. As you get familiar with our tools and systems, you can build upon them and tailor them to become your own for what works for you and your household. When looking at a situation or space in your home or office, here are some TLC Method questions to ask yourself and all involved:

- **Mindset: What is the current mindset?** What and who can improve the mindset to help us reach our goals? Do we need rest, nutrition, exercise, wise counsel, perspective change, and time on The Wondering Mat?

- **Tools: What are the current tools?** How can I apply the Earth Adventures For Kids tools for the better? Can I go to The Marketplace and find more tools to better the situation and/or space?

- **System: What is the current system affecting this situation or space?** What is the mode of operation? What and who can improve the current systems? Are the systems organized, functional, and efficient? How can we transform this situation and/or space through organization?

- **Marketplace: What are the problems and where can we find the solutions?** Go to The Marketplace and find solutions that become tools for you to add to your toolbox. Seek and you shall find. Become a solution hunter. Find your mentors and networks of people who can help.

THE BIG PICTURE . . .

Tackling everyday challenges when 1) raising kids and 2) providing care for others, is a skill that can be improved. Our book *How to Create Your Own Signature Collection: The Ultimate Guide to Improving Your Life and Legacy* is the first book in our series of books and contains all the "saving grace" tools we used when raising our kids, working with other kids of all ages, and providing care for others. Let's note that providing care for others must include our own self-care!

Ironically, as we aged and our parents aged, we discovered our books and tools help with elderly parents, too. This led us to create the second book in our series, *How to Create a Treasure Legacy Collection: The Ultimate Guide to Living Your Best Life Now.* The beginnings of this book were rooted in having young children and wanting to have a complete estate plan that went beyond the traditional sense of estate planning. We are each unique and each person is wonderfully made, with extraordinary ways, gifts, and talents including having an exceptional spirit and essence. We created the Treasure Legacy Collection as a way to embody all this amazing wonder of who you are into an encapsulating system that will make your life better now while leaving a legacy that will live on after we each pass on from this earth.

ORGANIZATION IS KEY IN APPLYING THE TLC METHOD.

When people hear the term "get organized" many people want to run for the hills and hide. Let's face it, dealing with our "stuff and piles" in the many spaces we function in every day is often viewed as a "dread" with a "someday I will do it" mentality. Dealing with our own "stuff and piles" allowed us to create new spaces and new ways of doing things that led to amazing results—improving our lives and legacy—and now we share it all with you, so you too can experience your own "transformation through organization."

Through our series of books, we teach you how to optimize organization in your home, office, and finances while improving relationships, quality of life, and building your legacy. **Thirty years in the making, our TLC Method includes books that unlock the door for new ideas and inspiration to help in all areas of life.**

Using our TLC Method, you can:

- ✓ Develop your signature lifestyle.

- ✓ Improve your mode of operation.

- ✓ Supercharge your parenting and caregiving.

- ✓ Live your best life now while building your legacy.

It's you, but better!

- **The two foundational books:** 1) *How to Create Your Own Signature Collection* and 2) *How to Create a Treasure Legacy Collection*, are both available now for immediate digital download, and make sure to also order a copy in print from Amazon. We recommend having both the digital download and the professional hard copy of each of our books from Amazon, as they will be your guide with printable worksheets and checklists, plus they will be part of your TLC for future generations.

- **From chaos to calm:** Our books show you the tools you need to have better days and nights, better relationships, and more.

- **Organize and thrive** in your home, office, and finances, while improving relationships, legacy, health, wellness, and quality of life—we cover it all.

- **Adult kids of elderly parents: Do you help take care of your parents?** Our books and tools can help you, too. Read *How to Create a Treasure Legacy Collection* today!

- Go to www.EarthAdventuresForKids.com or at ForParents.EarthAdventuresForKids.com for the additional TLC Method books and tools to help with your journey on the road to success.

- **Need extra help?** Sign up for our low-cost monthly subscription or our one-on-one 90-day Coaching Programs at ForParents.EarthAdventuresForKids.com; just scroll down to the coaching section.

Note: As parents, grandparents, and caregivers, we recommend you pre-screen our website content and books for your own decision of whether you think it is a rating of G, PG, or PG-13 depending on your own values, perspectives, and stages the members of your household are in at this time. For example, when kids are younger, sometimes we do not want to introduce certain topics until they are older. For this reason, we recommend you pre-screen our content on website pages, in books, and in our Journal Stories and decide what info you want to use with members of your household and at what times and stages. Please read and accept our disclaimers and release of liability in the copyright section of each of our books. By continuing to read our books, you acknowledge and confirm that you accept our terms and conditions including our release of any liability.

Read our books with a highlighter so you can easily highlight information you want
to reference later, including any action steps you want to take. Our books are guides and you can use them as working copies, so we recommend that for each of our books, you buy the digital download and the professional hard copy from Amazon.

Terms and Conditions and Release of Liability: If you decide to act upon any of the information presented in our books, tools, website, and so forth, you acknowledge that you have abilities, skills, knowledge, and responsibilities that are your own. The ideas and options presented by Earth Adventures For Kids are not advice, and you need to seek your own professional counsel and advisors. By going forward with reading and using any ideas, tips, information, and so on in the Earth Adventures For Kids books, including use of tools, systems, marketplace, and so forth, you acknowledge that you accept your sole personal responsibility for all results, consequences, risks, and liabilities, and you hold harmless the team at Earth Adventures For Kids and its affiliates, of whom you release from any liability.

All the best and aloha every day,

The Team at Earth Adventures For Kids

CHAPTER 1

WHAT IS A TREASURE LEGACY COLLECTION?

**Many may ask, "What is a Treasure Legacy Collection?" and
"What do you mean I can send my tender, loving, care to others through it?"**

Well, over the years, the team members at Earth Adventures For Kids have had their fair share of dealing with tough stuff in life, including the hardships of experiencing the loss of a loved one and the grief that comes with it. This topic is not easy to deal with; yet, over the years, through the difficulty we have had brightness peek through—kind of like the splendor of splintered sunlight that shines through a deep, dark, forest, and the sun sends rays of light through the dark.

Like our other books, this book, too, has grown like a lotus flower out of the mud, beauty from ashes, the best of things grown out of the worst of things. Not that this book will ease any pain of loss or promise any miracles, but it could show some ways to extract a richness out of those difficult times.

To be clear, we're talking about death but choose not to say the words we all dread hearing. So, we refer to this whole topic as "estate planning" or "life planning" and "sending your TLC with our TLC" through your legacy lifestyle using our TLC Method. Similarly, we have chosen to describe the passing on of our dear ones as something beautiful and amazing in ways that include words such as paradise, bliss, Promised Land, nirvana, future life, utopia, and so forth. This book is not about beliefs; those are your choices in how you view this topic of passing on. So, we will leave that here and get on to what our Treasure Legacy Collection is about.

The Treasure Legacy Collection is a way of life, building a "fullness of you" and "fullness of loved ones" estate plan that goes beyond the common legalities of the standard will and living trust. The acronym for tender, loving, care, and Treasure Legacy Collection is the same—TLC. So, we say we are "Sending our TLC (tender, loving, care) with the Earth Adventures For Kids TLC (Treasure Legacy Collection)." Through the pages of this book, we will tell you how you, too, can weave your tender, loving, care throughout the days of your life as strands and cords that help bridge the gap between Heaven and Earth.

In Ecclesiastes 4:12 from the New International Version of the Bible, we read, "Though one may be overpowered, two can defend themselves. **A cord of three strands is not quickly broken.**" A "cord of three" references a bond between you, God, and a loved one.

The Treasure Legacy Collection is about creating "cords" between you and a loved one(s), whether the people are present on this Earth now or have passed on. The cords between you can be in many forms; this concept is a significant part of this book. The Treasure Legacy Collection is about creating cords between us that bridge the gap between Heaven and Earth. In the process of creating cords, we also improve the quality of our lives and improve present relationships. **It is important to note that even if a loved one has passed on, we can still create the cords that bridge the gap between Heaven and Earth as we create a Treasure Legacy Collection in a loved one's memory.**

Estate planning is not usually an easy topic to discuss. But when you need it, well, it is wonderful when it is completed. Maybe you have a trust, a will, or some form of keepsake shelf or box. Because of the time it takes, the topic, the expense, and other unpleasantries involved, it is easy to ignore this important life plan and never get around to it.

This book is a guide to living your best life now with our TLC Method, complete with quizzes, checklists, and worksheets you can print now through the digital book download. Just print them, put them on a clipboard, and follow the steps—you can begin today! The process can seem daunting, but we have found that progressing through the stages of creating a Treasure Legacy Collection with our help is manageable, enjoyable, and very rewarding. We have additional coaching options to help you create a Treasure Legacy Collection and you can learn more at the end of this book in the coaching section.

YOU MIGHT SAY, "I ALREADY HAVE AN ESTATE PLAN."

★ **Chances are if you DO have a trust and/or will,** the components of your estate plan are scattered, disconnected, and are considered unpleasant topics that make it difficult to communicate with your loved ones.

★ **Chances are if you DO have a trust and/or will,** the entire "fullness of your essence," which refers to your being, your spirit, your uniqueness, your mojo if you will, is not being presented and shared.

In addition to making your estate plan comprehensive and integrated into your legacy-building lifestyle, this book will show you ways to capture the "fullness of essence" for you or a loved one and enjoy the present times together, creating the cords that bind and strengthen relationships. And when we, or they, depart this Earth, the cords remain as a comfort to those still on Earth, bridging the gap between Heaven and Earth.

Our TLC Method is bringing tender, loving, care into our way of life. Apply our TLC Method to change situations and spaces for the better. The practices and activities in this book are powerful and profound ways we have found to help us overcome feelings of sadness, grief, loss, uncertainty, trauma, and so forth. Each person has unique experiences, and we are simply sharing what has helped us. You can choose to add to your TLC lifestyle what you like and what works for you.

When we apply the TLC Method to a situation or space, we do the following checkpoints in this sequence:

1. Mindset—how do I see this situation and/or space? Do I need a perspective change?

2. Tools—what tools are we using? Do we need to find more tools to help fix the situation and/or space?

3. Systems—how are we using tools and how does mindset affect our mode of operation, beliefs, and actions? Do we need to change things up to get better results?

4. Marketplace—what is possible? Ask others who have had success in this situation and/or space. Are there products and services in the marketplace that can help us? Become a solution hunter. Seek, and when you find, apply the solutions as tools, and add them to your toolbox for success in life.

Are you looking for ways to:

✓ Bring more meaning, joy, and peace of mind into **today** and your present relationships?

✓ Bring more meaning, joy, and peace of mind into your future and the future of your loved ones?

✓ Get organized around your home, office, and finances?

✓ Leave an awesome legacy that comforts those as they continue on in your essence?

Read on to learn how to live your best life with the TLC Method and experience your own transformation through organization.

CHAPTER 2
WHY CREATE A TREASURE LEGACY COLLECTION?

Send your "TLC" tender, loving, care with our Treasure Legacy Collection (TLC). By using our Treasure Legacy Collection and our TLC Method, parents and grandparents, and anyone who is looking for a way to send their "TLC" tender, loving, care, and legacy into the future and beyond can also achieve organization, peace of mind, focus, meaning, better relationships, and better communication with loved ones.

As a parent, I often had to deal with the complex and uncomfortable difficulties of explaining to my kids the parts of life that I didn't want to deal with, such as the unexpected loss of a loved one and all that goes with it. As a mom, I would prefer not to have it as part of my kids' childhood. But again and again, we were dealing with those difficult questions about life and death and wondering how to go forward into a joyful future. The loss, the emotion, the turmoil, and the ecosystem of all the loved ones still here on Earth, wondering how to go forward without the loved one(s) here with us—how could life go on in a positive way?

We created the Treasure Legacy Collection and TLC Method out of a need to comfort my kids and me. **Knowing I could do things now** to help my kids and loved ones in the possible event of my own unexpected departure from this Earth inspired me, and we build on our TLC every day as a way of life.

Like us, do you hope to communicate to your loved ones in your estate plan ideas for celebrating you and maintaining your essence and your spirit that will help comfort them in your absence? If so, read on.

**Estate plans, wills, and living trusts cover the basics and necessities.
But we have found that we want to:**

★ include more to convey the heart and soul of ourselves and our loved ones and

★ use the TLC in a powerful way to improve communication, relationships, and quality of life now.

We want to include in our TLC all that we love, our favorites, our go-to wisdom, and our ways of life that make us who we are. We do this by writing down our favorite songs, TV shows, places, foods, family heritage, and so on. Writing down these favorites and keeping them in an organized, easy-to-access, enjoyable format is the basis of our Treasure Legacy Collection. We make this process easy by helping you create your "5 TLC Legacy Lists" with our books as your guide. We will discuss our 5 TLC Legacy Lists throughout this book.

It is common to procrastinate and avoid discussing estate planning. Many people find the topic unpleasant, disrespectful, and maybe even rude. In our experience, ignoring the issues and not talking about this part of life was not a solution for us, as we were thrust into this realm when many of our loved ones departed this Earth unexpectedly and tragically. We had questions. We experienced grief. We wanted answers and to regain a feeling and sense of control out of the uncontrollable.

Most of the time, we were not the direct people dealing with the loss and grief, but we were the ones helping others with their direct loss and grief. How does one offer comfort and hope of healing in such a time of loss, grief, and despair?

Estate planning and experiencing the loss of a life on this Earth is unique to each person. The loss is profound and painful, without easy answers. Each situation is a part of life's unique mystery. Each life is special and full of wonder, and when it is gone, we feel a deep need and desire to find or offer comfort and somehow ease the pain. We desire to find meaning and purpose in circumstances, including finding and celebrating the meaning and purpose in the life on Earth that was lived and now has passed on.

We decided we would begin building our Treasure Legacy Collection as a way of life, and we discovered we were making our lives better now.

In addition to adding my essence, my spirit, my nature, and my mojo to my Treasure Legacy Collection, as a mom, I want to build my TLC now and share with my family those parts of life that I believe are essential and of value. I want to build and offer "comfort cords" for my loved ones that include ways of celebrating in my spirit when I am no longer on this Earth. I want to style my collection in my way, in a way that is my own. This Legacy Lifestyle gives me peace of mind, improved relationships, and quality of life as I live out my TLC daily.

No one knows YOU better than YOU do, and taking time to collect some special treasures of who YOU are and the legacy YOU want to leave while here, as part of an estate plan—in a way that is full of respect, honor, grace, and love—can be rewarding for you.

And when the time comes, this collection of your treasures, your favorites, and your wisdom—what we call your "TLC" tender, loving, care—may help ease some of the loss and grief for your loved ones and give support for the eco-system of people who care for you and your loved ones.

ACT NOW FOR A BETTER LIFE AND LEGACY.

What motivated me to act and create my Treasure Legacy Collection? It was the thought, **"What if I did not act?"** The thought of an estate plan not done—what will worst-case scenarios look like? The thought of your family, friends, and the whole ecosystem of loved ones not having direction in your absence, can motivate you to act now and begin your TLC today.

Don't miss the opportunity to create cords of comfort and share wisdom, joy, and your TLC. With our books and tools, learn how to:

★ live your legacy daily,

★ leave your legacy for future generations, and

★ improve your life today by creating your cords that bridge the gap between Heaven and Earth.

The two situations below are often seen after the loss of a loved one:

1) The Completed Estate Plan:
   You may already have a completed estate plan and think it is great.

2) The Non-existent Estate Plan:
   You may know you should have one but put it off as life gets busy.

The completed estate plan helps fill in the gaps of what should be done right after the loss, but it is often lacking in how to provide ongoing comfort and joy as time goes by and the dust of the initial shock of loss settles. Our Treasure Legacy Collection helps you create the comfort cords that bridge the gap between Heaven and Earth.

The cords remain ongoing, long-term so that loved ones on this earth feel a sense of connection with loved one(s) who passed on. This can help through the phases of:

• initial shock of loss,

• as they begin to move on, and

• as they move through life long-term.

• Remember, you can create a TLC in memory of a loved one as a way to create comfort cords to help you and others when experiencing loss.

The fact remains that we still miss those who have gone on, and we wonder how we can carry on in the best ways. The estate plan often has a bare minimum of information, lacking the essence and mojo of our loved one and lacking detailed instruction for how to carry on through life long-term as best we can in their absence. Our Treasure Legacy Collection fills in these gaps and shows you the steps to take on your own. Plus, our coaching options of a low-cost monthly subscription or a one-on-one 90-day Coaching Program will help if you want additional motivation, accountability, and clarity while creating a Treasure Legacy Collection for a loved one, in the memory of a loved one, or for yourself.

The non-existent estate plan often causes doubt and hardship. It is difficult to walk through this time, leaving loved ones totally guessing in most areas without answers and clues. The scenario of a non-existent estate plan and the guessing and searching for clues can leave more doubt and unknowns along the way. I don't think anyone intentionally wants this for others, but life gets busy, and this topic is not easy. Until now, with our TLC, discussing estate planning was not considered enjoyable. Remember, creating your TLC with our TLC helps improve relationships and quality of life today! So, look at it as enjoyable, meaningful, and a wonderful way of answering the question, "What should we do today?"

Use our quizzes, bullet point lists, checklists, worksheets, and coaching information to determine your course of action and create your TLC within the next ninety days, starting today.

Our Treasure Legacy Collection completes the picture of how loved ones can carry on in your absence in a way that is as thorough, detailed, and precise as you want it to be. The Treasure Legacy Collection and our TLC Method reduce overwhelm. Establishing and developing your TLC plan is manageable with easy-to-follow steps in our proven format. Our TLC creation tips and recommendations help you develop a "fullness of your essence" estate plan, starting today, right now.

Our format can help with issues such as:

✓ Ensuring the language that you use in your collection and documents is legible and easy to understand.

✓ Ensuring your TLC is fun and engaging so it improves relationships and quality of life today.

✓ Ensuring that your home, office, and finances are organized so your TLC is easy to identify, locate, and enjoy.

The Earth Adventures For Kids Treasure Legacy Collection is putting "life planning" into your estate plan

and breathing into it the enduring fullness of your energy, your essence, and your being.

CHAPTER 3

WHY SHOULD I FOLLOW THE EARTH ADVENTURES FOR KIDS TLC METHOD?

It's easier to get this important task done if you use our books 1) as your guide and 2) as prompts for your own ideas so you can add your own style to your TLC. Follow our checklists, and bullet point lists, plus use our worksheets and quizzes in this book to help you create your TLC and follow the TLC Method of Mindset, Tools, Systems, and Marketplace.

Creating your legacy collection takes some "know-how" in terms of organization skills, creativity, and self-reflection. These challenges make it all too easy to put off this vital part of life planning. **But what if you don't take the time** to complete an estate plan, including one that shows the "fullness of your essence?" Imagine scenarios in life if you do not take the time now to create the cords, including present and future scenarios. Quality of life and relationships are at stake.

Without our Treasure Legacy Collection TLC Method guiding you, you can try to think of all the points to cover, and ways to create your legacy, looking for the materials and the guidelines. However, this research takes time, and your results may be incomplete. Do you really have time to search here and there for the necessary information? Do you have the creative skills to complete this endeavor on your own? Do you have the time it takes to learn the skills and find the information to include? Consider the time it would take you to create the comprehensive system as an easy-to-manage legacy lifestyle. Instead of trying to do this your own way, just follow the simple steps outlined in this book that we collectively call our TLC Method.

As obstacles build up and often overwhelm us, estate planning becomes another looming task avoided. **Our TLC Method makes the process enjoyable as a way of life.** In addition, if you set out to create everything from scratch without our format, system, checklists, and tips, you'll be pulling time and energy away from other things in life. Take the easier route. Complete our quizzes, and use our bullet point lists, checklists, and worksheets included in this book to either "DIY" do-it-yourself or have us "DIWY" do-it-with-you through our coaching options of a low-cost monthly subscription or different one-on-one 90-day Coaching Programs.

Creating an organized, meaningful legacy collection, with joy and humor, that makes it easy and fun for you and your loved ones to take part in takes some talent mixed with some "know-how." Not many people can think of ways to create a legacy collection and keep it updated, relevant, easy to access, and enjoyable. Our research, thought, practice, and trial and error can benefit you.

We have often been in a position of loss and in a position of needing to comfort those experiencing direct loss, helping them pick up the pieces. We are not experts, and we are not perfect, but we have learned a few things along the way.

The stories of loss for us were all different, unique, often tragic, and unexpected. I had many experiences walking through this "valley" with my children and needing to comfort them, giving them guidance and light, and providing them with hope and ways to step out of those darker times. I noticed the same elements over and over again that came into play while helping those remaining here on Earth move beyond despair, we learned we could glean great meaning and great reward, and celebrate lives well-lived, harvesting beauty from ashes. The Treasure Legacy Collection and TLC Method help you create a legacy of your treasures, your wisdom, your joy, your guidance, and your comfort in an easy, organized, and enjoyable—yes, enjoyable—way.

Not knowing how to create your collection is one of the obstacles you can overcome with our help. Collecting your items for your "TLC" does not have to be a chore, and it does not have to be difficult to assemble. We have created the Treasure Legacy Collection checklists, bullet point lists, and worksheets in this book to help guide you and help you see your progression. The quizzes help you determine if you prefer DIY or DIWY.

The biggest step to take now is to commit to creating your Treasure Legacy Collection with our TLC Method and begin the steps to completion by:

1) printing out the checklists and the worksheets in this book.

2) printing the quizzes at the end of this book and doing them to assess your situation.

3) selecting and printing bullet point lists in this book you want to have for easy reference and reminders.

4) putting whatever you choose to print on a clipboard for easy access and reference.

I get it. Life is busy and demanding. We know we can only do so much. Creating your Treasure Legacy Collection can become another pressure on the "to-do" list. No worries! We have become so familiar with the tools in the Treasure Legacy Collection that we can easily incorporate the TLC Method into our days and nights as an effortless way of life. You, too, can get all the tools and become so familiar with them that you naturally incorporate them into your days and nights in an enjoyable way that improves your quality of life and relationships today.

We call it "Creating our Legacy as a Way of Life." It can be as simple as having intentional days and nights in which you do the activities, plan the experiences, make the phone calls, subscribe to the subscriptions, reach out, and do the things that matter to you in ways that work for you. You may do this already without even thinking about it, but by adding in our TLC books, format, checklists, worksheets, and quizzes, you can make sure you are including everything in your "legacy as a way of life" living.

If you follow our checklists, and bullet point lists, plus use our quizzes and worksheets in this book, in minutes, you can begin your Treasure Legacy Collection and continue to add to it, building on it daily in an effortless and enjoyable way.

Our goal is to create our Treasure Legacy Collection as a way of life, and we have become so familiar with the elements of the Treasure Legacy Collection and the tools within it that we just incorporate the actions into our daily lives. We have discovered that this "legacy way of life" improves our relationships and our quality of life. Get to know each tool in the TLC and become so familiar with it that incorporating your legacy building into your daily life is second nature.

MASTER THE TLC METHOD.

You can buy our digital download books to begin your TLC, print the checklists, bullet point lists, and worksheets, and then put them on a clipboard for easy reference. Follow the steps outlined in our checklists and worksheets to complete your TLC. Complete the quizzes to gain insight into your situation.

As you read through our content, practice applying the TLC Method—Mindset, Tools, Systems, and Marketplace—in your life and master the art of identifying components of a situation and/or space to see if the situation or space is humming along fine or needs change for improvement with the TLC Method. Learn to see if the situation or space can be improved by mindset, tools, system, or marketplace—often all of the above—and then take action in the areas you want to improve.

EACH BOOK IN THE EARTH ADVENTURES FOR KIDS SET INTEGRATES WITH OUR TWO FOUNDATIONAL BOOKS:

1) *How to Create Your Own Signature Collection* and

2) *How to Create a Treasure Legacy Collection*—this book you are reading.

You can buy all our books in print on Amazon. Buy them for yourself or as gifts to others. The digital copies are nice to buy too, because you can print the quizzes, bullet point lists, checklists, and worksheets to use. Each digital copy is good for one IP address. Share the links to buy our books with others so they too can enjoy creating their TLC as a way of life.

The Treasure Legacy Collection helps you ensure your "TLC" tender, loving, care and guidance, wisdom, and energy are captured and easy to access, enjoy, and pass on to others in your absence. You may have loved ones who play a significant role in your life, and you will want to ensure they, too, have created a TLC in case you need to step in at some point and assist them with important aspects of their lives, such as finances. For example, if a loved one gets sick or has an illness and someone else needs to handle everything for a time, it helps to have everything ready for a trusted party to step in and assist. It more than helps! It is often the difference between success and failure in making sure bills get paid, income gets processed, and essential paperwork is easy to find.

Does getting your financial information organized sound like another overwhelming chore? Just like the other parts of our lives improved with our TLC as a way of life, our finances also improved when we got organized in the financial and office space. Our book *How to Create a Financial Worksheet* makes it easy for you to get organized in your finances and reap the rewards!

The best estate planners and financial planners may ensure your legal and financial details are covered, but they may fall short when capturing the essence, energy, zest, and mojo that truly represents who you are.

You can use our tools, which were developed over decades of observing, advising, and comforting those who have gone through loss. Customize your own system with our tools to fit your unique needs and use our ideas as prompts for your own ideas. Investing in the Treasure Legacy Collection and implementing the system means saving time, money, and energy, and getting a return on investment (ROI) in the form of better relationships, more peace of mind, and increased quality of life. Completing the financial organization part of your TLC helps improve your finances due to organization and awareness of what is happening in your finances.

THE COST OF NOT PREPARING A "LIFE PLAN" WITH OUR TLC, CAN MEAN A LOWER QUALITY OF LIFE AND MISSED OPPORTUNITIES.

Our TLC Method offers a way to create at your pace, in your way, and in the detail you desire. Paying a professional organizer for their tips and tricks could cost much more. Although you might want to hire some assistance for some parts of the TLC creation that require time spent organizing, creativity, and talent in certain areas if that helps you. Maybe a friend, family member, charity, or church member can help with those parts of the TLC creation you need assistance with, and this experience together will further create memories that become part of your legacy as well. For example, ask a friend, volunteer, or family member with the skill, willingness, and ability in the area you need help with. Offer them a special dinner, outing, or a paid fee for their assistance.

Sometimes we must go solo in our endeavors, and we talk about going solo throughout this book, as going solo, when needed, is a pillar of the Earth Adventures For Kids mindset—we do what it takes and forge our own path.

EXPERIENCE THE POWER of communicating your mojo, essence, and energy into your TLC, including the power it has on your relationships and quality of life.

Age doesn't matter. You can begin weaving your Treasure Legacy Collection into your days and nights at any age, right now. The elderly, the middle-aged, the young parents, grandparents, and those who do not have children—*anyone* can create a Treasure Legacy Collection and live it as a way of life.

Even young adults may have read the book, *Seven Habits of Highly Effective People* by Stephen Covey, in which the author declares the importance of living with the mindset of "begin with the end in mind" as applied to many different projects, activities, goals, and endeavors—and ultimately applied to our whole life picture.

The Treasure Legacy Collection can define your way of going through an "intentional life well lived" today, as well as define your future way of going through life with your loved ones beyond your time on this Earth. How powerful is that?

AND EVEN MORE POWERFUL IS THE WAY OUR TLC METHOD IMPROVES LIFE TODAY, HERE AND NOW.

Ask yourself if you need direction on making this time on Earth more meaningful with loved ones. Do you need ideas on ways to increase your significant contributions to your loved ones' lives? We help you with this, too. Just do the following:

★ Write your 5 TLC Legacy Lists with our books as prompts. We explain this later in this book.

★ Use our checklists and worksheets to make your own action plans and take action in your life.

★ Ask others to join you in doing activities and creating your TLC as a way of life.

★ If you would like assistance, our coaching can help you. We offer a low-cost monthly subscription and one-on-one 90-day coaching.

★ You can also give our coaching programs to others as a gift, and if you like, make your TLC creation a shared activity, completing your TLC at the same time with another person.

To begin improving relationships and making your time with others more meaningful, you can simply invite your loved ones to participate in creating your Treasure Legacy Collection to increase your quality of life with them today. Our TLC Method helps you improve relationships and improve communications. Let this book *How to Create a Treasure Legacy Collection* be your guide.

Your Treasure Legacy Collection increases the quality of life now, suggesting:

• Activities to do now.

• Conversation topics for today.

• How to have meaningful conversations on life's values.

• Financial topics to discuss.

Are you looking for ways to:

✓ Increase the quality of your relationships today?

✓ Tell your stories to your loved ones and to the world?

✓ Pass on your treasured favorites to your loved ones and to the world?

Why not try our Treasure Legacy Collection system, designed with this in mind? Designed by me—a mom who has walked the walk through the valleys and up to the peaks, and who knows the challenges, struggles, and obstacles of overcoming the parts of life that deal with losing a loved one. I also know the struggles of strained relationships and how the TLC can improve these relationships.

Our TLC can help you create more tender, loving, care—TLC—in your life. You will get hundreds of ideas for activities and ways to create your legacy in a tangible, organized, and meaningful way. This will improve the way of life for your loved ones in your absence, and it will also increase the quality of the relationships and time you are spending together now.

During my kids' younger years, after dealing with loss, I wanted them to be comforted if I unexpectedly departed, so I taught them one of my favorite songs performed many times by the Jerry Garcia Band, "*My Sisters and My Brothers.*" You can look up the lyrics online to see why this song is included in my TLC.

I was comforted knowing that if I unexpectedly departed the Earth, my kids would know this song and sing it to self-comfort as I created this cord between us that would bridge the gap between Heaven and Earth. **This is the power of creating your TLC now with your loved ones—you can create cords of comfort to bridge the gap between Heaven and Earth.**

An example of the power of creating a TLC in a loved one's memory is the poem on a friend's memorial service card. The poem was printed on the card by his sons, in honor of their dad who passed on. I am not sure who wrote the poem, so I will not cite it here, but I will again highlight the power of the TLC created in a loved one's memory including a poem that declares 1) what they enjoyed doing together, 2) they will see each other again someday in Heaven, and 3) in the meantime, while his sons remain on Earth, they will wait and go on in his memory with his essence, spirit, energy, and mojo. How comforting! **I hope this inspires you to**

✓ Write the poems now.

✓ Have the experiences together now.

✓ Have meaningful conversations now.

Our Treasure Legacy Collection has hundreds of ideas to help you, including ways to be together now. Even though you may not even live in the same region, you can still share moments of togetherness.

For example, we recommend **getting a GrandPad device powered by Consumer Cellular for loved ones that you do not see regularly.** The GrandPad offers an easy way to stream music that is comforting and fun to share, as well as share photos and websites. We have one for each of our dads, and they LOVE streaming their favorite music from when they were kids. My eighty-year-old dad will call or text me just to let me know he is listening to Elvis Presley again or he is listening to some of his favorite gospel and hymns. The GrandPad has been a way of spending treasured time together even though we are not in the same region.

The GrandPad has many commercials online and they show how the elderly who experience music are comforted, and because of the music, memories return to their best times in life, giving a physiological response of joy, peace, calm, and wonder. We have a closer relationship by enjoying music together with our parents through the easy-to-use GrandPad. My father-in-law is in his 80s and he uses his GrandPad every day for news, music, and surfing the web. The simplicity of the GrandPad brings the most tech-challenged people into the digital world.

I recommend searching online for different GrandPad commercials

and then watching them to see how powerful these connections can be.

Another example of having shared time together even though we are in different regions is having the same monthly subscriptions to KiwiCo.com or a similar subscription service in which we receive the same items/activities, and we enjoy doing the activities and discussing them. In our experience, teenagers—yes, teenagers—enjoyed doing the monthly activity crates from KiwiCo.com and could share the experiences with their cousins and grandparents even though they all lived in different regions.

These shared experiences of togetherness, though apart, are a great gift of today's technological and Internet age; take advantage of it! I often think of how it was for our ancestors. When their loved ones left the region, they might never see or hear from them again. Letter writing and word of mouth traveling through others were the best ways they could communicate. With the Internet and technology platforms, coupled with delivery systems such as digital download, UPS, FedEx, USPS, and so on, we can be in close communication and relationship with our loved ones regularly even though we are miles apart.

Having these shared experiences with our loved ones even though we are in different regions is also creating "cords of comfort" with our loved ones as a way to bridge the gap between Heaven and Earth. We can think of Heaven and Earth simply as different regions!

Use the power of the digital age to improve relationships and communication. You can also use the power of recording messages to keep messages forever. For example, do an online search on how to store voicemails and preserve them for the future. You can use recordable storybooks to help bridge the gap between Heaven and Earth, plus keep a connection when you and loved ones are in different regions on Earth. You can search online for ways to use voice recordings, including adding recordable books to your TLC by Hallmark and other companies. On the Hallmark website, the section on Recordable Storybooks at www.Hallmark.com says:

"Storytime with the kids in your life is a favorite part of the day for many moms, dads and grandparents. You can create memories for a lifetime by sharing favorite kids books together. But there are days and times you can't be there for story hour. With Hallmark's recordable books, you can still read their favorite books to them, even though you're far away. Whether you travel for work, are stationed overseas in the military, or are a grandparent who lives in a different state, recordable storybooks for children help you share a favorite bedtime tradition even when you're away. Just press the record button to record your voice. Personalize your story with silly voices and personal messages to the child. If you mess up, you can record a page again. Children will cherish the magic of hearing your voice when you're far away so even when you're apart, these books will bring you closer."

In addition, missed moments that life offers us are missed opportunities to create a meaningful legacy. Now is the time to start practices that promise to create more meaningful memories. It takes effort. Consider the past. Do you want more of the types of experiences you have had? Do you want better, more meaningful experiences in your future? None of us are perfect, and we all have limitations, but going forward, set your goals for what you want to achieve and accomplish.

Creating a Treasure Legacy Collection that is unique to you helps you transition easily from now to the future. It bridges a gap so that in the event of unexpected loss, a bridge between Heaven and Earth is present, and hopefully over time, reduces the sense of a deep divide. The unexpected and unplanned event of losing a loved one with us on Earth often creates a state of despair. We're left guessing how to fill the gap, especially with younger children. My goal as a young mom raising kids was to somehow find a way to create cords of connection in the event of my absence.

CHAPTER 4

THE MANY APPLICATIONS FOR TLC

The Treasure Legacy Collection can also be used in other cases of absence related to time away for any reason—divorce, travel, health issues, incarceration, and more. The Treasure Legacy Collection is a way to help those who feel the loss of the presence of a loved one deal with those moments in which they say, "I need you here. I miss you. I love you. Until we meet again."

The Treasure Legacy Collection helps fill the void of those difficult feelings. It creates comfort cords, bringing direction, guidance, healing, inner strength and fortitude, and ways to carry on with the spirit and essence, the mojo of the person(s) we are missing. Learning to self-comfort gives one a sense of control. It taps into a supernatural power that overcomes the situation, allowing us to experience victory and joy in difficult circumstances. It helps us rise above.

I have found that implementing the TLC Method of Mindset, Tools, Systems, and Marketplace with our tips, habits, practices, and disciplines can also help **deal with types of loss such as break ups, divorce, loss of a job, foreclosure, and any other loss that comes with hardship, change, disappointment, upheaval, and a sense of "failure."** It is important to note that the appearance of failure does not mean all is lost. Out of failure comes many good things, such as lessons learned, new beginnings, and so forth. We can still experience feelings of loss through perceived failure and have the need to process the experience and let it go, looking forward and moving on. The Treasure Legacy Collection TLC Method can help with this reset and renewal phase after many types of loss.

Using the tools in the collection helps us go from shock, grief, despair, sadness, and anger to find inner strength, resolve, inspiration, and more. Using the tools helps create a future vision and helps us take practical steps to go from point A to point B. Sometimes people get stuck in a mental and emotional state and need help moving beyond the experience of grief, mourning, anger, regret, doubt, and fear that may have resulted from various experiences. We at Earth Adventures For Kids are not professionals; we're just sharing what has worked for us.

Sometimes professional help is required, and sometimes self-help is key. Each person is unique. Our Treasure Legacy Collection has the tools that have helped us, and still help us, move past these areas of strongholds. We show you what we do to move beyond, rise up, and win. Your journey is your own, but we hope some of our tools help you, too. The following are just some examples of how we used our tools to help a situation for the better.

HOLIDAY EXPERIENCES
changed for the better through TLC:

As a young mom with no one coming to holiday celebrations such as Thanksgiving and Christmas, my inner strength and fortitude, with divine inspiration, helped me to say to myself, "It is just us for the holiday, and we will make it the most special occasion as possible." The TLC tools helped us focus on what we did have rather than focusing on what we did not have, allowing us to create new traditions and experiences tailored to our family. Holidays and the expectations they bring, the feelings of missing out or not having what we want, can all play a part. The Treasure Legacy Collection can help!

It has been said that "imagination rules the world," and I like to **employ both imagination and inspiration for uplifting and extraordinary results.** So, we used some simple techniques to make our holiday special, and what we started back then has become a way of life and our new traditions. We have since added to our tradition-setting, and each year as we are able, we make holidays even more exciting, adding in a little swanky touch when we can—such as going to a spa resort for Thanksgiving week—and now, more and more family members are joining in the fun, and planning their Thanksgiving holiday with us at the resorts. One place we often go has a tradition of building a 5-foot-tall gingerbread house made of real gingerbread and thousands of pieces of real candy. Their tradition has become our tradition, and we can play games by their fireplace and smell the 5-foot-tall gingerbread house nearby. Super cozy! It takes planning—like booking early and setting money aside each month—but the results are worth it!

When life gives you lemons . . . make punch!

Our "punch" tradition started one year when my kids were little, and no one was coming for the Thanksgiving or Christmas holiday. At that time, our daughter was going through a normal phase of nighttime anxiety experienced by many people in the winter. We decided to actively engage in all the community seasonal events that included lots of lights, singing, music, food, plays, and so forth. We read every local publication we could and mapped out our winter holiday festivities. We went to three different church candlelight services in one day and the services often included cookies and carols which added to the festivities. We went to many free and low-cost performances. That was the year I started my true appreciation for what has become known as "the ugly Christmas sweater" because it brought color and fun to a dark time.

We started our own holiday tradition of making what we called "Christmas Punch." We bought a beautiful, red, acrylic punch bowl and random ingredients such as pineapple juice, pineapple rings, bubbly water, and various juices. The kids each made their own punch. They had fun pouring and slicing fruit and then drinking the punch from fancy wine glasses. The colors of the punch, the fruit, and the punch bowl were all very uplifting.

The punch was different every time we made it, depending on the ingredients. To this day, we still enjoy our holiday punch which can be made at any time—just give it a special name like "New Year's Punch," "Thanksgiving Punch," or "Valentine's Punch," depending on the holiday. It brings a smile to our faces to say it. And we love saying "punch bowl" by giving a fun, light punch to the arm and then making a bowl with our hands. Try it! Give a light punch to the arm and make a bowl with your hands really quick and say "punch bowl" at the same time you do the actions.

We have great memories of this simple tradition we created. As parents, we were modeling how, despite the darkness of winter, in the absence of relatives, even with the extra challenge of some anxiety, we just went on in the spirit of "the best of the season." Through this, we were weaving new traditions, creating new memories, deepening relationships with others, and engaging in building local community—and I hope my kids will continue this holiday punch bowl tradition after I have departed this Earth, as a way of continuing on in my spirit and mojo.

In the holiday seasons thereafter, we shared our traditions with others and always got a laugh and enjoyment from the whole experience. Making punch seems like a thing of the past, from the 1950s-'60s, but we brought it back for our family, and you can, too. Experiment with high-quality, whole-blend ingredients.

BECAUSE OF OUR TLC WAY OF LIFE, WE CREATED THESE NEW WINTER HOLIDAY TRADITIONS:

★ Watching different versions of the movie *A Christmas Carol*, adding in Will Ferrell's new twist on this old tale called *Spirited*, which in our opinion, is an amazing example of bridging the gap between Heaven and Earth.

★ Seeing every possible winter music performance, such as sing-alongs, caroling, choirs, bells, and more.

★ Going to every possible holiday function at schools, churches, and theaters, and giving where we can.

We created our own "fullness of the season" by making our own way. We were successful because we applied the TLC Method of Mindset, Tools, Systems, and Marketplace. We have learned to use inspiration and imagination to overcome all sorts of states of mind and emotion. These experiences teach us that we are like a tree planted near the water. We can thrive and flourish as we tap into the life-giving "water" that feeds us, and we grow strong and produce beneficial fruit.

When we see this picture of our roots and choose to tap into a stream that feeds us in good ways, we gain confidence and clarity, including knowledge of where to go when we need that inner strength, fortitude, and inspiration. From this, we can grow an ecosystem like the picture of the tree on the cover of our book *A Series of Unsuspecting Children's Poems*. The roots, the trunk, the branches, and the ecosystem that grows out of them represent health and life flourishing for generations. You can view the book cover at ForParents.EarthAdventuresForKids.com and at www.EarthAdventuresForKids. com under the Shop sections.

The power of The Wondering Mat:

Think of The Wondering Mat, an item in our TLC, as a place where you plant your feet, tap into your stream of inspiration, and grow your inner strength and fortitude, which will produce beneficial fruit for you and others. Like the mountain pose in yoga, this is about centering yourself, building your foundation, getting alignment and harmony, connecting, and moving through the physical world with your inner self in harmony.

The Annual Newsletter Becomes a Family History Book

Another tradition arising from the question, "What are we going to do this holiday season to mark the time and make it special?" was writing my annual newsletter.

You can do this too! I started writing a one-page reflective summary of our past year's highlights, challenges, themes, and goals achieved. Every December, I look back over the year and see what reference points stick out, for good or bad. Some years I have included Old World, multi-cultural winter holiday traditions passed on through the ages that we still keep today, including their origins, and special recipes. I laminate the newsletter every year; it is often double-sided. From this tradition, which started when the kids were young, we now have a twenty-page family "history book" that grows yearly.

Reading through the pages of our annual newsletter family history book each year has become another tradition we look forward to every winter. I know that in the event of my absence, my family will have comfort in the words of wisdom, the stories, traditions, and recipes passed down from me to them. In recent years, I have shortened it to a Christmas card collage with our typed newsletter on the back. I like using Snapfish for this, but many alternatives are available. I used the Costco photo collage option and made larger collages when the kids were younger. These are fun ways to view many photos at one time easily, and we bring them out every winter season, keeping them the rest of the year in our Save Forever Boxes marked for holidays.

Overcoming feelings of sadness during the winter holidays is a struggle for many. We have found that reframing the holidays to spend time at a spa over Thanksgiving has helped! One year, instead of exchanging presents, we stayed at Hotel Del Coronado in Coronado, CA where they had ice skating and fire pits with lots of holiday fun indoors and outdoors. This is part of our decision to have more meaningful experiences rather than having more "stuff." We treat ourselves and just enjoy, taking time to have meaningful conversations. Use the Treasure Legacy Collection tools to rise above whatever challenges you face, no matter the season. Identify an area you would like to overcome. Define your goals and achieve them.

People often compare themselves to others or covet what others are doing, especially in this day of social media sharing. Feelings of inadequacy, deficit, or fear of missing out (FOMO) may creep in.

I encourage you to look back over the last season and the last twelve months and remember the high points, the low points, and what growth came out of these times. Learn to see big things in small things. You can practice the skill of "reframing situations" in the best light.

When you begin to self-reflect, see what transpired in your last season, and then celebrate it, you're on your way to living a joyful life. Self-reflection brings gratitude, praise, and thanksgiving. Reggae music is often great at giving thanks and praise! Play some Bob Marley songs and read the lyrics. Many of Bob Marley's songs are inspirational and they are about overcoming. Music—in the form of hymns, gospel, choir music, good old rock 'n roll, or whatever you like—helps you transcend difficult circumstances. Another song we love is called "It's A Beautiful Day," sung by The Kiffness and Rushawn which you can find on YouTube. The song celebrates all that life is, the good, the bad, the ugly. Singing and finding joy in all things is a strength, and it is contagious.

Practice the art of reframing situations in life into the most positive light. It might take some effort, but it is a skill that can be improved upon with time. Make it second nature to see the glass half full. Practice by looking at a situation you currently interpret negatively in your life. Then, turn it into a positive by intentionally changing your perspective.

I attended a conflict resolution program through a local mediation organization, and we learned the art of reframing situations—practicing reframing in many different situations. Through a shift in perspective and focus, we can change circumstances for the better and improve relationships and quality of life. This training has helped me immensely in life and I think it is a good idea for everyone to take some sort of mediation training.

In the article *Reframing: The Essence of Mediation* by Peter Blanciak, the author states, "Psychologists and therapists have long used a technique called reframing to assist patients with changing problem attitudes and behaviors . . . . There are many ways to do reframing. Zoub mentions quite a few of these; included are: rephrasing, focusing, proposing an option, moving from abstract to specific, going behind positions, stimulating new ideas, looking to the future, dealing with emotional outbursts, preempting, creating a metaphor, offering choices, involving the quiet participant, assigning homework, being direct, using a ludicrous intervention . . . ." https://mediate.com/reframing-the-essence-of-mediation/

A Chinese proverb about judging whether things are good or bad in a circumstance is illustrated on this website: https://www.linkedin.com/pulse/parable-chinese-farmer-what-taoists-can-teach-us-hodges-ed-d- The farmer chooses to wait and see how everything unfolds, rather than judging something as bad or good. Similarly, a guiding principle we live by is the Bible scripture that tells us God works everything out for good.

When we talk about our concept of coming to terms with it all—the good, the bad, and the ugly—we choose to reframe situations in the best light and take the good, learn from the bad, and move forward with intentions and new growth for a productive future.

Maybe when reflecting on your last year, and the last previous years, there are situations you need to reframe in order to move forward in a positive way. You can decide to make the next year more intentional by choosing activities to create your Treasure Legacy Collection with loved ones and even solo.

SOLO ACTIVITIES

Solo activities are just as rewarding and beneficial as doing activities with loved ones. Writing this book for me is a solo activity. I have many solo activities that are rewarding and beneficial.

One of the foundations of the Earth Adventures For Kids mindset lies in the power of solo activities and solo intentional living because it deals with having the attitude that no matter the circumstance, I have a choice, and I choose to see this situation in a positive light and I choose to do "＿＿＿＿＿＿" fill in the blanks. By having this resolve that no matter the circumstance, I see it positively and I am doing positive activities and "thinking good thoughts," then, you become what I call a "pillar in society."

A pillar in society is defined by Collins Dictionary as "A person who is universally respected-reliable-decent and hard working that is more of a giver than taker; often engaging in voluntary work and taking up worthy causes who neighbors and the community have high regards and esteem for."

When you decide to live your TLC as a lifestyle, you become a pillar in society, and you can seek to help others as well. Our coaching programs can help with this process, and you can learn more about becoming a Certified Earth Adventures For Kids Lifestyle Coach to help others with their TLC Method and Legacy Lifestyle. For more information, visit ForParents.EarthAdventuresForKids.com and scroll to the coaching section. Remember, Earth Adventures For Kids is for everyone—you don't have to be a parent. As we all know, we each have parents, so every person is part of "parenthood" in some way because we all have parents!

Get the calendar out and book some new things to try. The Treasure Legacy Collection can be a wonderful motivator and a way to look forward to future seasons. The annual winter newsletter family history book I mentioned above is part of my unique Treasure Legacy Collection; adding to it has become a way of life for me now. You can do this too!

Your daily life can become a lifestyle of creating your TLC:

1) through solo activities—meeting people along the way.

2) in the name of your loved ones—creating cords of comfort.

3) with loved ones—improving relationships.

Your system of creating your Treasure Legacy Collection becomes an enjoyable way of life. The initial setup can be challenging, but our books and tools guide you, making it manageable.

Creating your Treasure Legacy Collection is as easy as:

★ Reading our books and downloading the digital books, then printing the quizzes, checklists, and worksheets to use as your guide.

★ Keeping our printed quizzes, checklists, and worksheets on a clipboard to easily reference.

★ Getting your containers ready to fill with your favorite items.

★ Buying our labels and marking your containers and journal/binders with our TLC labels.

★ Adding into your containers and journal/binders what you want as part of your TLC.

The steps are simple, and your daily life will benefit from you taking these action steps. Living the TLC lifestyle does not make life harder; it makes life easier! You don't need to be a professional estate planner, financial planner, author, or photographer to use our system. You don't need to know anything about professional organizing. You don't need to be a good communicator.

Our format and tips can help you get started, cover all your important topics, and do so in a way that keeps you from getting sidetracked, and being scattered, and helps you get everything into a manageable system that works for you. We help you get your 5 TLC Legacy Lists written, your stories told, and your home, office, finances, and life working harmoniously in an upward spiral. You can be ready for life's challenges, like a parkour moving through an obstacle course—you can deal with whatever you encounter.

IMPROVE YOUR RELATIONSHIPS TODAY.

Another area the Treasure Legacy Collection can help in is the realm of difficult, and maybe even broken, relationships. In some cases, people may have difficulty with estranged loved ones or resistant and complex, strained relationships with loved ones. Again, we ask ourselves in this realm of relationships, how can we apply the TLC Method of Mindset, Tools, Systems, and Marketplace to have better outcomes? There are infinite possibilities, and your TLC will differ from others' TLC, as we are each unique and every situation and space is different at different phases of life.

The beginning of creating your "TLC" with our "TLC" can be as simple as an announcement to loved ones that you are starting a legacy project and building your legacy as a way of life. If there have been strained relationships, you can request that bygones be bygones or ask to let issues be water under the bridge. Then ask them to join you in creating your TLC. In the case of relationships in which you may not be able to build bridges of trust or communication, you can simply include well wishes in your collection, and maybe they will find them in your TLC later in life.

In some cases, relationships can be improved. Healthy boundaries and trust with goodwill are essential, and by creating your TLC, you may come to terms with your worst scenarios and reframe them into best-case scenarios and resolutions. You may help lay to rest issues of struggle. Even if it is the simple act of writing down something and placing it in your TLC Save Forever Box and then moving on. Letting go will free you to enjoy your life.

No one wants broken relationships, but they happen. And in our best ability, we can try to mend relationships, but in the cases in which, for some reason or another, those relationships cannot be mended at this time, you can use your "TLC" with our "TLC" to set a best-case scenario for goodwill and possible reconciliation later.

This is an opportunity to address issues and leave some problems in the best light possible according to your perspective. Try to reframe the situation, see the other's perspective, or maybe revisit the issue later. But for now, recognize you can only do so much, and you need to move on with your own purposes for your own life that is more in your control.

If a loved one has already departed this Earth, create a Treasure Legacy Collection to honor their spirit and memory. Invite others to join you in creating this TLC and define the items, traditions, and favorites included in this loved one's TLC.

Sending your TLC with our TLC means multiple results for the same effort. For example, when you write your 5 TLC Legacy Lists and use these lists as part of your Legacy Lifestyle, you can use the same 5 TLC Legacy Lists in the following ways:

1) **as tools for intentional living**, giving you ideas for activities to do today and this weekend, et cetera.

2) **as the basis for writing and preserving your stories** to share with others. We use our 5 TLC Legacy Lists as launching points for writing our stories to include in our TLC.

3) **as a way to create cords of connection** and bridge the gap between Heaven and Earth so others know how to carry on in your essence, spirit, and mojo in your absence. This is done by using the lists to do activities together, and then keeping the lists in your TLC Save Forever Box and TLC Journal so others can carry on in your essence, in the event of your absence.

OUR TREASURE LEGACY COLLECTION TLC METHOD GIVES YOU THE FOLLOWING:

★ Dozens of ideas on how to leave your favorites in many areas of life for your loved ones—bridging the gap between Heaven and Earth.

★ Ways to communicate your zest for life and what makes you **YOU**—directing others how they can go on in your spirit and essence in your absence, creating cords of comfort that help to comfort them when you are not present.

★ Steps to take to get the system in place with appropriate containers for all the joy and wisdom you will leave in your legacy.

★ Ways to help put into words those difficult things to communicate.

★ Ways to collect and create photos and other memorabilia.

★ Ways to tell your loved ones how they can best remember you and what you love in life—creating cords of comfort in the event of your absence.

★ The power of now and translating this moment of now into improved relationships and improved communication with those you love.

★ The power of you in the future, with ideas on what loved ones can do in the future to celebrate you, including starting a foundation in your name, starting a regular fundraiser/memorial, and telling them how you want to be remembered, such as going to your favorite park or beach, listening to your favorite music, and eating your favorite foods.

★ Ways to enjoy your collection with tips to make your TLC clear, concise, legible, inspiring, easy to access, motivating, and comforting.

★ A format to follow with easy steps to take. The hardest part will be dealing with the "stuff and piles" and mastering the art of sorting and deciding which items to keep, toss, recycle, repurpose, sell, and give away. We give you tips on getting through this part of the TLC later in this book.

★ Ideas for containers and our labels so that your new space can handle the incoming, outgoing, and storage for that space.

★ Steps to write your 5 TLC Legacy Lists and use these lists 1) as tools for intentional living 2) as the basis for your stories and 3) as a way to create cords of connection and bridge the gap between Heaven and Earth.

★ Ways to get your stories and history preserved in easy-to-access formats that are enjoyable for you and others including photos of items associated with the stories.

★ Ideas on how to use video and digital methods in your TLC that will allow your legacy to have a presence here on Earth forever!

★ Ways to use the power of the TLC Method of Mindset, Tools, Systems, and Marketplace to be wildly successful.

A WORD ON THE POWER OF THE MARKETPLACE:

Parents, family, and friends are often the people we go to when we need help or support, including wanting to share good news, challenges, and "just talk." In life, we often need to be "solution hunters" and seek out remedies for "pain points" in life. When key people in our lives are no longer there for one reason or another, it can be difficult, to say the least.

We have used The Marketplace to find not only remedies to problems of all sorts, but to also find our tribe—our communities of support, our mentors, and have shared experiences within those communities. We join email lists, we reach out, we get involved and we get notified of what is happening in different spaces. With technology today, we can take part in events such as webinars, Zoom calls, virtual events, in-person events, and more. The ability to chat with others, share resources, celebrate achievements, help others, discuss challenges, and so forth is key to living your best life and living your legacy daily.

The Marketplace includes our Earth Adventures For Kids online marketplace, plus whatever marketplaces you encounter, seek, and find in your local community and in your life, wherever you may be, online or in the physical world. The Marketplace includes for-profit businesses, non-profits, churches, clubs, charities, various organizations, and basically anything in the "public square," also called the "town square" where people come together to buy, sell, and share ideas, resources, knowledge, and give and get support.

DISCOVER THE POWER OF ENGAGING WITH THE MARKETPLACE AND BRING IT INTO YOUR LEGACY LIFESTYLE.

REAL PEOPLE BENEFIT FROM THE TLC METHOD

While it may seem like an estate plan couldn't improve lives today in the here and now, I've been amazed at how the TLC has improved users' lives with:

★ new habits and disciplines.

★ organization of home and office.

★ improved relationships and finances.

★ better communication with loved ones.

From Pat in Boise, ID—Mom of Nan, founder of Earth Adventures For Kids:

"Before using the Treasure Legacy Collection organization system, my treasures were buried beneath a lot of stuff, and many wouldn't even know they were treasures. With the 90-day TLC Coaching Program, in a short time, I was able to bring out those treasures, share with others why they are treasures, and place them into containers and shelves where they can be protected, appreciated, and enjoyed. I was able to organize my writing, streamline my financial picture and key info, and learn to keep up with these systems on a weekly basis. Creating my Treasure Legacy Collection not only cleaned up my house, my office, and my finances, but it also gave me time with loved ones to discuss my treasures in life and to have peace of mind that I am not leaving them a mess. I enjoy a more organized household every day! Fortunately, everything was in place when I unexpectedly was hospitalized with the coronavirus, and my loved ones could easily step in to manage my affairs for two months. When I went on the ventilator, and they did not know if I was coming back to my home on Earth or going to my heavenly home, they were comforted knowing my Treasure Legacy Collection made everything more manageable and eased the pain of saying, 'Until we meet again.'"

One comment I received on the Thanksgiving spa/resort tradition:

A family told me that they are so thankful they took the time to enjoy a family retreat for a special holiday. They had a great time with lots of photos taken. Little did they know it would be their 70-year-old husband and stepfather's last with them on this Earth. The months that followed were difficult with his unexpected passing, but the memories of their recent retreat as an extended family helped and still help comfort them all; the pictures will become part of their TLC.

27

Ash, Ani, and Andrea on their mom's creation of her TLC as a way of life during their childhood:

"Our mom started creating her Treasure Legacy Collection when we were kids. Every year she created an annual newsletter around Christmas time, laminating it, and now we have a history of our years as kids. We have the framework for what to do if, God forbid, she departs our Earth before we are ready. We have ways to celebrate her life here with us—like, as she says, 'cords of comfort bridging the gap between Heaven and Earth.' We know her treasures, and where they are so we can appreciate them. The Wondering Mat can be used in her memory with prompts printed on it that give us inner strength and resolve. The TLC books can give us energizing activities to carry on in her spirit and tap into her mojo. The Financial Worksheet can help us so we are not left without means for provision, and we'll know how to create and build our own financial structures. The Financial Worksheet helps us manage the finances if needed. The Treasure Legacy Journal/Binder keeps all her favorites and wisdom pieces she wants us to know in life. The Marketplace gives us additional wisdom and choices for bettering our lives and finding solutions to problems. And we know she has sent us her 'TLC,' so we feel that vibe and sunshine when we use The Wondering Mat and the other tools in the system. The TLC Save Forever Box has all her keepsakes and mementos she wants us to have. Everything is in an organized system that is easy to access and store, and we enjoy everything in a simple way that is not burdensome or overwhelming. It's a way of living that has improved our relationships and quality of life."

Noel on Creating a TLC in memory of his Grammy:

"After Grammy passed, we discovered in her treasures that she was photographed by Dorothea Lange in 1933, and the portrait is at the Oakland Museum of Art. We also discovered more of her rich Hawaiian heritage, finding her relatives' history in many Hawaiian books at the Bishop Museum. I inherited some of the family dinnerware from the 1800s, a collection of wooden and coconut bowls. We do not have a clear, written family history of our own, so using the TLC as a guide, I have pieced together some of the histories and I am creating a TLC in her memory. I am including certain historical books documenting our family contributions, the info on the portrait by Dorothea Lange, and pictures of our family heirloom collection of coconut and wooden bowl dinnerware from the 1800s.

"We are creating a TLC in her name so that it can live on for our family in future generations, including possibly donating the dinnerware to the Bishop Museum in Honolulu and visiting her portrait in the Oakland Museum of Art. We will make a family trip to Oahu, hire a professional photographer, and create videos documenting this experience. Had she created a TLC in her own words and in her own way, we would have more information, such as her connection to Dorothea Lange and so forth. In this TLC process, I have talked more with relatives and created experiences we may not have had if we were not creating this TLC. I recommend that every person begin creating their own TLC today, as each person is unique and special, and has a rich story to tell and share. And in the process, I am sure your present life will benefit from going through the TLC process and living TLC as a way of life."

Not buying and using the Treasure Legacy Collection could mean:

- Leaving a "mess" for loved ones as they search for information and guess, trying to piece together items.

- Living in an unorganized household with buried treasures your loved ones may or may not find.

- Missed moments for building better relationships, more positive memories, and increasing quality of life.

- Feeling regret over the missed opportunities.

- Feeling frustrated over disorganized finances, papers, and lost treasures.

- Wondering what can be done and guessing instead of being confident and knowing.

- Settling for lower standards and fewer meaningful experiences.

Because the Treasure Legacy Collection is such a valued system that helps people now and, in the future, the money invested in buying the tools in the Treasure Legacy Collection seems insignificant in terms of the return on investment (ROI) you get in the form of better relationships, better communication with loved ones, and increased quality of life.

Better relationships, increased quality of life, organized finances, and a more organized office and household help you have better days and nights. The Treasure Legacy Collection helps you on the path to achieving your goals today.

IN THE EVENT OF THE PASSING OF A LOVED ONE WHO DID NOT CREATE A TLC, YOU CAN CREATE ONE FOR YOURSELF OR FOR OTHERS, IN THEIR MEMORY.

Creating a TLC in a loved one's memory can be healing and comforting. It can provide ways to enjoy a loved one's essence, being, zest, and mojo in your own way that is unique to you and your relationship.

Just buy what you need from our Treasure Legacy Collection list to use in their name and memory, such as a container for their TLC Save Forever Box marked with our TLC Save Forever Box label. Put memorable items of value for remembering your loved ones. You can self-direct activities to do in their memory and invite others to join you. Create TLC Legacy Lists in their name and ensure that their essence, zest, and mojo live on for others to benefit from and enjoy.

You can also give others our Treasure Legacy Collection as a gift. Compile all the parts of the TLC like our hard copy books from Amazon and place them in a labeled TLC Save Forever Box. Give the TLC to them as one set. The container you source can be as long as The Wondering Mat if you like, so the mat and everything else will fit inside. Use the checklists and worksheets included in this book as your guide. Consider giving others our coaching programs as a gift as well.

CHAPTER 6

HOW TO START YOUR TREASURE LEGACY COLLECTION

To begin your Treasure Legacy Collection, read through the following checklist and print it to use as you go through your TLC process. Having all our books both digital and published from Amazon is ideal because you will want to print the bullet point lists, checklists, and worksheets to use, plus have the professionally printed version of our books to keep in your TLC Save Forever Box. After you print the checklists and worksheets, put them on a clipboard to keep handy for quick reference as you move through the stages of creating your TLC and living your legacy lifestyle.

CHECKLIST OF OUR PRODUCTS FOR YOUR TLC TRANSFORMATION THROUGH ORGANIZATION

☐ **READ OUR BOOKS AND WRITE YOUR 5 TLC LEGACY LISTS.** Create and implement your own action items based on the information in our books.

1) **Foundational Book 1:** *How to Create Your Own Signature Collection: The Ultimate Guide to Improving Your Life and Legacy*

2) **Foundational Book 2:** *How to Create a Treasure Legacy Collection: The Ultimate Guide to Living Your Best Life Now*

3) **Book:** *101 Things to Do Other Than Social Media*; use it to write your Activities in My Name List

4) **Book:** *A Series of Unsuspecting Children's Poems*; use it to write your Values and Pillars List

5) **Book:** *How to Create a Financial Worksheet*; use it to write your Financial Nuts and Bolts List

6) **Book:** *When the Sun Goes Down: How to Enjoy the Night*; use it to write your Cozy and Comforting Nights List

7) **Book:** *Earth Adventures For Kids Fitness*; use it to write your Health and Wellness List

8) **Marketplace Annual Access Membership:** Use it to write your Health and Wellness List, Values and Pillars List, Financial Nuts and Bolts List, Cozy and Comforting Nights List,

and Activities in My Name List. The products and services found in The Marketplace will give you ideas on important information you want to add to your 5 TLC Legacy Lists.

☐ **BUY OUR LABELS AND SOURCE YOUR CONTAINERS.** Containers with proper labels are key to getting organized. Buy our labels and source your containers.

9) **Label:** Save Forever Box—this is explained in our Signature Collection book.

10) **Container:** Save Forever Box—this is explained in our Signature Collection book.

11) **Label:** TLC Save Forever Box

12) **Container:** TLC Save Forever Box

13) **Label:** TLC Journal/Binder

14) **Container:** TLC Journal/Binder

15) **Container:** The Catch-All Bag

☐ **BUY OUR WONDERING MAT AND USE TO RENEW, RESET, CALM.**

16) **A Tool for Transformation:** The Wondering Mat with the TLC, can be used during times of remembering your loved one(s) allowing profound inner experiences to take place.

☐ **GET YOUR MEGAPHONE FOR EFFECTIVE, FUN COMMUNICATION.**

17) **A Tool for Communication:** The Megaphone with the TLC, can be used during the "sorting and deciding of the stuff and piles" process. Make it fun! Read our book *How to Create Your Own Signature Collection: The Ultimate Guide to Improving Your Life and Legacy* for more information on how fun and powerful The Megaphone can be. **We recommend that the megaphone is only used by caregivers and adults; kids can respect this as an important tool.**

☐ **REACH YOUR GOALS FASTER WITH OUR HELP.**

18) **Get coaching help with our low-cost monthly subscription, webinar group coaching events, or our one-on-one 90-day Coaching Programs.** We help you use our TLC Method to reach your goals and improve your life and legacy! Go to our website page at ForParents.EarthAdventuresForKids.com to learn more.

Here are more details on each part of the TLC products listed above:

1. **This book you are reading now,** *How to Create a Treasure Legacy Collection*, is the beginning of learning what is involved in the legacy lifestyle, our TLC Method, the tools, and the steps you can take.

2. **The Wondering Mat,** as part of your TLC, is where you tap into your stream of inspiration and imagination. It is a space to refresh, regroup, and remember loved ones who have passed on. You can use The Wondering Mat as a place to read our books, make your lists, and plan your Treasure Legacy Collection actions and activities. There are unlimited uses for The Wondering Mat. Kids will especially appreciate this special place to remember their loved ones if they have experienced loss, and their caregivers and mentors can model how to use The Wondering Mat as a place of healing, overcoming, imagination, meditation, and inspiration.

3. **The TLC Save Forever Box and its Label** are about the containers, giving a place to sort items and store items. The box is for treasures, keepsakes, stories, photos, mementos, and a place for you to store our TLC books and your 5 TLC Legacy Lists that you will generate from our books.

   Our Label is key! Do not underestimate the power of using our label on all containers for your TLC. The label easily communicates to you and others that the container has items of importance that are part of a collection. Proper labels that match make it easy for you to identify that the containers are valuable and part of your TLC. Even if you have different types of boxes/containers for your TLC, they will all be made uniform by having our label affixed in an easy-to-see place on the box. Anyone can quickly and easily identify that the boxes are a collection of important items. Buy our labels on our website at **ForParents. EarthAdventuresForKids.com** or **www.EarthAdventuresForKids.com** today.

   For ideas on sourcing your TLC containers and TLC Journal/Binders, consider your décor, budget, and vision for the space you are creating. Just make sure that our labels can be adhered to them. Visit websites such as IKEA, Pottery Barn, Home Depot, The Container Store, Grand In Road, California Closets, World Market, Costco, and so forth to get a vision of what you would like to create with your storage containers.

   When possible, Earth Adventures For Kids will source everything in the TLC for you and ship it as one set for your convenience. In the meantime, you can source items on your own. Many people like to source their own containers/boxes to match their style, décor, and space. Using our labels to properly identify the containers and journal/binders is essential as they communicate that the containers are a valuable part of a Treasure Legacy Collection.

4. **Catch-All Bags** as part of your Treasure Legacy Collection are versatile containers for any items needed/used in the interim process of creating your TLC. They are also used for quick access to the items stored inside, plus they have a "take and carry" feature for on-the-go.

   For example, we have our formal estate plan in a Catch-All Bag right now as we work to compile and update our trust and will. Catch-All Bags make it easy to take out the items and put them all away when we are done working so we don't have cluttered piles of stuff around the house. We also have a different Catch-All Bag holding our tax documents, as we will be working on taxes. Using Catch-All Bags helps us keep categories and projects separated, quickly identified, and stored for easy access and easy put-away, all in a festive, appealing bag that brings us joy.

In addition, use Catch-All Bags to easily carry The Wondering Mat and other items on an outing to remember your loved ones. This can be especially powerful for kids who have experienced loss, as they may want to go to a special park or another location that the loved one(s) they miss enjoyed going to. This is a way to carry on in their loved one's spirit. Caregivers and mentors can model the use of the tools as they teach the child to use Catch-All Bags and The Wondering Mat as part of their loved one's tender, loving, care (TLC) sent to them.

You can use Catch-All Bags in countless ways as part of your TLC. Caregivers and mentors can help kids be mindful of the TLC practice. You can see more pictures of our Catch-All Bags in use at www.EarthAdventuresForKids.com on the Shop page. Send us pictures of your Catch-All Bags that you sourced and show us your pictures of how you use them for organization and for doing activities.

Use the "nesting bags" concept we discuss later in this book to make your days and nights better by being organized, versatile, quick in responses, flexible, ready to go, and able to handle many situations with your system of "nesting bags" using different sizes of Catch-All bags, Ziploc bags, Parker Clay bags/purses, and other bags that work for you. This helps you keep separate categories and keep like-items together with protection of the items, making them easy to find, access, use, and so forth instead of spending valuable time rummaging through loose items trying to find something you need.

5. **The TLC Journal/Binder** is a place for papers, wisdom pieces, and important information. You can add a section for pertinent financial information and have a separate binder just for accounts and passwords. Your annual, laminated newsletter can be added as a separate collection of your writings. Your TLC Legacy Journal/Binder can be kept in your TLC Save Forever Box(es). Our labels will identify to others that your Journal/Binder is part of your TLC. Do not underestimate the power of using our labels to identify critical parts of your TLC, as it will communicate to your loved ones in your absence that the containers are part of your TLC. Buy our label for your TLC Journal/Binder at **ForParents.EarthAdventuresForKids. com** or at **www.EarthAdventuresForKids.com** under the shop section.

6. **The Marketplace,** as part of your TLC, is a place in which to connect with other communities, find your tribe, find products and services that make your life better, and direct your loved ones to do the same. You can find products and services to enjoy as shared activities, shared subscriptions, and shared products. Embark on the journey of experiencing these activities, products, and services together as a way to find remedies for pain points in life, and improve quality of life, relationships, and communication.

7. **The Megaphone** is a fun and effective way to communicate with others on outings and while doing the sort-decide-thru-the-stuff-and-piles phase of organizing in your home and

office. We recommend megaphone use only for adults; kids can respect it as a tool used by caregivers.

8. **TLC Legacy List 1 of 5: Our book** *101 Things to Do Other Than Social Media* as part of your Treasure Legacy Collection is a checklist, a guide, and an inspiration for your own ideas in creating your **Activities in My Name List.** Store the list in your TLC Save Forever Box or TLC Journal/Binder with our label affixed. Use it to let others know what they can do to carry on through life with your spirit, essence, and mojo. You can get ideas from the book and tell others what you want them to do in your name. We have listed activities in The Marketplace so make sure to join The Marketplace.

    For example, we went to Six Flags amusement park in my aunt's name, and we visited other amusement parks in my grandparents' name after they had passed on because when they were here on Earth with us, we did this activity together. We all enjoyed a day together, remembering our loved ones. And I have directed my loved ones to go to Knott's Berry Farm in my name—especially at Christmas time.

    The book suggests ways to spend time together now, creating memories and creating cords of comfort. We can remember loved ones, do things they enjoyed, and continue to do what we did together. Include the book in your own TLC Save Forever Box(es) and add to it if you like. Tailor the list to your style and use the book as a launch point to create your own list of activities. This book can be especially powerful for kids who have experienced loss. They can take part in activities in memory of a loved one.

9. **TLC Legacy List 2 of 5: Our book** *A Series of Unsuspecting Children's Poems* as part of your Treasure Legacy Collection is where you think through, ponder, and self-reflect upon your values and what words of wisdom you would like to pass on to your loved ones. Through the lens of TLC, this book serves as a checklist and a guide with prompts for writing down your ideas and thoughts on what is important in life as your loved ones carry on in your absence. Include this book in your TLC Save Forever Box(es) and add to it, using it as a prompt to write your own piece on your values, your pillars of strength, and the important parts of life you will want your loved ones to know.

    Use this book to generate your **Values and Pillars List** to keep in your TLC Save Forever Box or TLC Journal Binder with our label affixed. This book can be especially powerful for kids who have experienced loss as they can learn key value points from their loved ones, and kids can use this book to create a TLC in memory of a loved one. Use this list to have meaningful conversations.

10. **TLC Legacy List 3 of 5: Our book** *When the Sun Goes Down: How to Enjoy the Night* as part of your TLC is a way to address the special role of nighttime and all that it can bring. Sometimes the night is a time of deep soul-searching and moments that may not occur in the day when we are busy with other things. You can use this book as a guide, a checklist, and for ideas and prompts on how you would like your loved ones to be comforted, cozy, and inspired during the night. Use this book to generate your own **Cozy and Comforting Nights List.** This book can be especially powerful for kids who have experienced loss, and caregivers and mentors can help kids use this book when making their way through the

hours from twilight to dawn. Store your list in your TLC Save Forever Box or TLC Journal Binder with our label affixed. In this book, we include tips on improving sleep with solutions we have found. We have listed our best sleep improvement solutions in The Marketplace so make sure to join The Marketplace.

11. **TLC Legacy List 4 of 5: Our book *How to Create a Financial Worksheet*** as part of your TLC is a place to give financial structure to build within and give hope for the future. It is a place to communicate and deal with assets, liabilities, goals, visions, priorities, and more. If there is a lack or a need, it can be a place of prayer and thanksgiving, an act of "setting out the jars" of faith for blessings to come in and "fill the jars." The concept of filling the jars is from a story in the Bible in which a widow had nothing. She prayed and was inspired to collect as many empty jars as possible. She borrowed jars and was amazed when they were supernaturally filled with oil she could sell.

Finances are often a place of stress and avoidance, but the book is powerful, and the benefits are sure to amaze. Use this book to generate your own **Financial Nuts and Bolts List** to communicate the financial aspects of life you find important to communicate to your loved ones. If you do not yet have a Financial Worksheet, create one and keep it current. Inform your loved ones that you have developed this Financial Worksheet as part of your Treasure Legacy Collection and explain to them how you use it daily, weekly, monthly, and yearly and that it will be there for others in case they need to access it in your absence. Keep a copy of your Financial Nuts and Bolts List in your TLC Journal Binder with our label affixed.

12. **TLC Legacy List 5 of 5: Our book *Earth Adventures For Kids Fitness*** as part of your TLC is used to write your **Health and Wellness List** which can include your best remedies for ailments, ways to be healthy and well, lifestyle tips for quality of life, and more. In this book, we include ways we regained health including losing weight, gaining muscle, and supercharging our nutrition to improve our lives. We have listed health improvement solutions in The Marketplace so make sure to join The Marketplace. Store your list in your TLC Save Forever Box or TLC Journal/Binder with our label affixed.

RE-CAP ON HOW TO GET STARTED:

✓ **Learn the components of creating your TLC,** a "fullness of your essence" estate plan that gives love, guidance, comfort, key information, and wisdom, while capturing your zest for life and passing that on to your loved ones in your absence.

✓ **Buy all the tools** listed in the TLC, including the books, and read them! Place the books into your TLC Save Forever Box, TLC Journal/Binder, or Catch-All Bag. Buy your containers, TLC Journal/Binders and buy our labels. With our labels on the (TLC) Save Forever Box and TLC Journal/Binder you will easily communicate to others that they are your TLC.

✓ **Follow the action steps** you want to take in our books, checklists, and worksheets. We like to highlight our action steps with a yellow highlighter so we can easily reference what we want to do. From your digital copy of this book, you can print all the checklists, bullet point lists, quizzes, and worksheets and keep them on a clipboard to easily reference.

✓ **Define your Mindset, Tools, Systems, and Marketplace** for the situations and spaces of life you are working in. Is everything helping you, or are there components that are hindering your results?

YOUR 5 TLC LEGACY LISTS ARE GENERATED USING OUR BOOKS.

1. Write your **Activities in My Name List** generated from the book *101 Things to Do Other Than Social Media*. Keep the list in your TLC Save Forever Box or in your TLC Journal/ Binder, both marked with our labels.

2. Write your **Values and Pillars List** generated by the book *A Series of Unsuspecting Children's Poems*. Keep your list in your TLC Save Forever Box or TLC Journal/Binder, both marked with our labels.

3. Write your **Cozy and Comfort Nights List** generated by the book *When the Sun Goes Down: How to Enjoy the Night*. Keep your list in your TLC Save Forever Box or TLC Journal/Binder, both marked with our labels.

4. Write your **Financial Nuts and Bolts List** generated by the book *How to Create a Financial Worksheet*. Keep your list in your TLC Save Forever Box or TLC Journal/Binder, both marked with our labels.

5. Write your **Health and Wellness List** generated by the book *Earth Adventures For Kids Fitness*. Keep your list in your TLC Save Forever Box or TLC Journal/Binder, both marked with our labels.

A note on typing:

It is best to type your TLC Legacy Lists and all your TLC writings as it makes it easier to edit and add to them, and it is easier for your loved ones to read. Over time, ink or pencil will fade, so it is best to have typed lists. If typing is not easy for you, have someone type them for you.

Laminating your typed creations can have amazing results! You can laminate your creations and TLC Legacy Lists to add more protection. I go to stores such as Staples and The UPS Store for all my laminating.

Type up printed directions to guide your loved ones on the parts of our books that mean the most to you and make your own notes from each book, using our books as idea prompts for writing your own to-do activities. We can help you with this through our low-cost monthly subscription or our 90-day Coaching Programs.

A note on the importance of using The Wondering Mat in the TLC Method:

Develop a practice of inner strength building and meditation by using the Wondering Mat. Use it to build your inner strength and fortitude to become a pillar for yourself and your loved ones. Use it to transform the body, mind, and soul, and share these experiences with your loved ones. You can buy The Wondering Mat for loved ones so they, too, can have these experiences. Inform them that The Wondering Mat practice can be used for many purposes, including in your absence when they miss you and seek comfort.

Knowing how to calm yourself, focus, use your imagination, and receive inspiration on The Wondering Mat is a powerful way to overcome challenges in life.

Play some music you enjoy. Try the free Pandora music platform and experiment with their different radio stations. Turn it up! Learn to relax on the mat. I turn up the music, lay flat on my back, and roll a tennis ball up and down either side of my spine, upper, mid, and lower back. I learned this technique thirty years ago from Peter Sterios, https://levityoga.com/peter-sterios-welcome-and-biography/ now a world-renowned yoga guru. It is very therapeutic, relaxing, and calming as tension is released!

As we say in our household, "Fill your love cup," which we see as the hole in each person's heart that needs "divine in-filling." Use the mat to listen to music or a podcast, read scriptures, read your wisdom pieces, and write your 5 TLC Legacy Lists and notes from our books. Teach others the art and skill of self-comfort on The Wondering Mat. Kids can especially benefit from this practice of learning to self-calm and comfort on the mat.

MORE INSPIRATION ON WHAT TO WRITE IN YOUR TLC . . .

In addition to writing your 5 TLC Legacy Lists generated from our books, you can define and write down your additional interests, attitudes, values, behaviors, actions, and habits that helped you achieve good results in your life and what you recommend to your loved ones to continue on in your spirit and legacy. The books will cover all these topics, but you can expand on your TLC Legacy Lists as much as you like.

Type up these notes so they are easy to read. The typing process helps you fine-tune your message, making it cohesive, organized, and concise writing to speak to future generations. You could write about how you helped someone overcome a challenge or how you overcame a challenge. Try to keep entries to one page, depending on the topic.

If you need help with writing, ask for assistance from a friend or relative, maybe take a writing workshop, or explore using writing software and artificial intelligence such as Chat GPT, Write Sonic, or Automatic Script by Doodly. Canva.com has also added a writing tool. You can use Grammarly.com to edit and help write your stories.

Community colleges and adult schools often have low-cost workshops that can help you learn how to use the technology and learn writing skills. Online "how to" videos may also help, and we will be posting helpful videos on our website as well. Join our community at www.EarthAdventuresForKids. com to **get on our email list to be notified of new releases, updates, and "how to" videos.**

Check out Storyworth at https://welcome.storyworth.com/ —a great tool to help you write your stories. From their website: "Everyone has a story worth sharing. Preserve meaningful moments and memories in a beautiful keepsake book. Then, share the experience with loved ones and discover stories you never knew." Storyworth has a great systematic approach to helping you write your stories.

We also have ways to help you write your stories. Go to ForParents.EarthAdventuresForKids.com and www.EarthAdventuresForKids.com to learn more about:

★ our low-cost monthly subscription service to help you create your TLC, write your 5 TLC Legacy Lists, and Tell Your Stories.

★ one-on-one 90-day Coaching Programs to help you create your TLC, write your TLC Legacy Lists, and Tell Your Stories.

On our websites, go to the coaching section to learn more about how we can help you stay focused, move through the process in a manageable way, get your 5 TLC Legacy Lists written, your stories written, and get your TLC done and incorporated into your daily lifestyle with ease.

SOME QUICK-REFERENCE USES OF OUR TOOLS THAT YOU CAN BUILD UPON:

1) **The Wondering Mat** - Use for building inner strength, and fortitude, igniting joy, using imagination, reframing situations into the most positive light, receiving inspiration, and using it as a place to go to remember loved ones who have passed on.

2) **The TLC Save Forever Box** - Use it for sorting items and identifying items of value and treasures, pulling them out of clutter, and placing them into this storage box for future use and enjoyment by loved ones in your absence. Your TLC Save Forever Box can include storage for photos, treasures, mementos, the Earth Adventures For Kids books, your TLC Legacy Lists, and more. **Buy our TLC Save Forever Box Label** and mark your TLC Save Forever Box as such for easy identification.

3) **Catch-All Bags** - Use them for quick access to items. These bags are easy to carry, and help you get organized by separating projects and activities. They provide a way to make it easy to go through your "sorting-and-deciding-of-your-stuff-and-piles" process discussed later in this book. Categorize items that are part of your Treasure Legacy Collection creation. We use Catch-All Bags for temporary storage when completing large projects such as creating a TLC, doing taxes, or estate planning. Use different sizes of free-standing Catch-All Bags for the "nesting bag" concept of "bags within bags" to manage your "stuff and piles" and help you make quick "sort and decide" decisions. With the nesting bags, you will be ready for a variety of situations at a moment's notice.

4) **The TLC Journal/Binder** - This binder holds key information and wisdom pieces you want to pass on to others. As my mom reminded me after her parents passed on from here on Earth with us, you cannot ask them when they are no longer with us, so it is good to have important information in a place that is easy for key people to access. Buy our TLC Journal/Binder Label and mark your TLC Journal/Binder as part of your Treasure Legacy Collection.

5) **Labels for the TLC Save Forever Box and TLC Journal/Binder** - these are key to getting organized because they make all your storage in boxes and binders uniform and easy to identify as part of your TLC.

6) **The Marketplace** - You'll find our marketplace on our website at www. EarthAdventuresForKids.com under Marketplace. You can browse the aisles online and see what companies have helped us improve our quality of life and relationships. Write down directions to your loved ones on how to use our Marketplace to find comforting, quality products and services to help them in their days and nights. Store your written directions in your TLC Save Forever Box. Use The Marketplace to find your tribe and communities you resonate with. Also, use The Marketplace to find products and services that can be used to bring people closer to others with shared subscriptions and shared purchases.

You can add these products and services to your 5 TLC Legacy Lists to inform others that you recommend them. For example, I want my kids to know about my favorite healing salves and my other go-to supplements that give relief for different things. You can also send us your favorite products and services and we will see if we can add them to The Marketplace.

7) **The Megaphone** - Use a megaphone as a fun and effective way to communicate with others on outings and during your "sort-and-decide-through-the-stuff-and-piles" organizing process. We like smaller-sized megaphones with a strap and volume control. We recommend megaphone use only for adults; kids can respect it as a tool used by caregivers.

8) **Book: *101 Things to Do Other Than Social Media*** - Store this book in your TLC Save Forever Box marked with our TLC Save Forever Box label. Make notes on activities of special importance to you and use the book as a prompt for creating your own **Activities in My Name List** to direct others on activities they can do with you now and in your name in the future. You can direct them on how to carry on in your spirit when they need comfort and need to feel your love. For example, as mentioned above, when my aunt passed on, we went to Six Flags Magic Mountain together in her memory, as she loved to go there. I have instructed my loved ones to go to Knott's Berry Farm if they want, especially at Christmas time, in my memory because I love that, and we have enjoyed going there together. Store your **Activities in My Name List** in your TLC Save Forever Box or TLC Journal/Binder. Use the list to do activities.

9) **Book: *A Series of Unsuspecting Children's Poems*** - Store this book in your TLC Save Forever Box marked with our TLC Save Forever Box label. Use the book as a guide to create your own **Values and Pillars List** and writings on important parts of life. Note which values and pillars in the book are the most important and valued by you. Offer any experiences or wisdom in each area and create your own list of what you believe to be important values

and pillars of life. Store your Values and Pillars List in your TLC Save Forever Box or TLC Journal/Binder. Use the list to have meaningful conversations.

10) **Book:** *When the Sun Goes Down: How to Enjoy the Night* - Store this book in your TLC Save Forever Box marked with our TLC Save Forever Box label. Use this book as a prompt to create your own **Cozy and Comforting Nights List.** Store this list in your TLC Save Forever Box or TLC Journal/Binder. Use the list to do activities and help you and others have a wonderful time from twilight to dawn.

11) **Book:** *How to Create a Financial Worksheet* - Store this book in your TLC Save Forever Box marked with our TLC Save Forever Box label. Inform your loved ones that you have compiled all your financial information into your TLC in case they need to step in to assist in an emergency. The Financial Worksheet helps you keep organized on important aspects of finances in general. Inform loved ones on what they need to be aware of in your finances and build in risk management like life insurance and other ways to help provide for your dependents in the event of your absence. Using this book, generate your own **Financial Nuts and Bolts List.** Store this book and your list in your TLC Save Forever Box or TLC Journal/Binder so others will be able to access your important financial information and wisdom. Use this list to take action on important items.

12) **Book:** *Earth Adventures For Kids Fitness* - Store this book in your TLC Save Forever Box marked with our TLC Save Forever Box label. Use the book as a guide to create your own **Health and Wellness List** and store the list in your TLC Save Forever Box or TLC Journal/ Binder so others will know your important health wisdom, tips, and remedies. Use this list to do activities and have meaningful conversations.

13) **Book:** *How to Create a Treasure Legacy Collection* - Use this book as a guide and follow the steps included and discussed. Pick and choose what works for you and incorporate your own unique ideas. Inform your loved ones that you are creating a "TLC" to send your "TLC" to them. Bring loved ones into the process and enjoy the improved communications, improved relationships, and the prompts to help facilitate discussions on otherwise difficult topics. Identify each item in the Earth Adventures For Kids Treasure Legacy Collection for its purposes and use them! You will find new ways to use them as well as the ways we have outlined in our books. Become familiar with the tools and their many uses, and you will discover that the tools and systems have many applications and integrations that can help you in life.

RECAP ON THE LEGACY LIFESTYLE AND TLC METHOD:

- ✓ Buy each part of the TLC, including the labels for your TLC Save Forever Box and TLC Journal/Binder.

- ✓ Become familiar with each tool in your TLC system.

- ✓ Inform your loved ones that you are creating a TLC to send them your TLC. Invite them to join you in any part you wish. You can go solo on any part or all of your TLC.

✓ Read all our books and write your 5 TLC Legacy Lists from them.

✓ Use all our tools and create systems unique to you and your needs.

✓ Take all the steps outlined that work for you.

✓ When each part of your TLC is established, learn how to incorporate it into your days and nights and add to it as you go through life, so living your TLC becomes second nature and a way of life.

✓ Continually invite your loved ones into the process if you like. You can also decide to go solo on activities if others are unable to join you, or maybe you prefer solo TLC activities.

✓ Adopt a lifestyle of creating your legacy every day.

✓ We offer a low-cost monthly subscription service and one-on-one 90-day Coaching Programs if you want assistance creating a TLC and living the TLC lifestyle with our TLC Method.

✓ Apply the TLC Method of Mindset, Tools, Systems, and Marketplace to situations and spaces.

✓ Consider signing up for our coaching options, including the option to become a Certified Earth Adventures For Kids lifestyle Coach to help others create their TLC using our TLC Method and Legacy Lifestyle. Learn more in the coaching section of this book.

CHAPTER 7

TECH SAVVY ANYONE?
DISCOVER THE WONDERS OF TECH

A t this point in the tech revolution, especially after experiencing the *"corona-shut-down-mass-technology-training-for-all-generations,"* we all at least know what the Internet is capable of and how the platforms can be used for amazing endeavors that get amazing results.

Since 2020, we have all had to get past some "mental blocks" of using tech. I know many eighty-year-olds who are savvier than I am on social media platforms and smartphones. Age is not so much of a factor as is being able and willing to learn. My 80-year-old dad told me, "I am not able to really operate on the Internet." I have felt the same way, and I am thankful that many platforms and devices now have plug-and-play ease of use, similar functions, features, and user-friendly, intuitive ways to generate excellent results and help us accomplish our goals.

So, let's put on our "can-do mindset" and think about applying our tech skills to our TLC to make this process fun and get amazing results. Just as many of us had to learn to use Zoom, order grocery delivery online, and get meals from local establishments ordered online—often against our will but out of necessity—we can approach two of my TLC tech recommendations in the same way—seeing it as essential and necessary because the rewards are worth it. Be willing to ask for help when needed, practice, and get the job done.

MY TWO TECH RECOMMENDATIONS ARE:

1) **Use Canva Pro:** Make presentations, collages, videos, greeting cards, and more with your photos and videos. Type your stories, TLC Legacy Lists, and wisdom pieces, adding headlines, images, and more.

2) **Digitize Your Print Photos:** Take pictures of old photos with your smartphone and send them to your email and to your loved ones' smartphones.

USE CANVA PRO:

Discover the joys and ease of Canva Pro. Go to www.Canva.com and look around. You don't have to be a designer or marketing business professional to utilize Canva. Canva Pro is a worthwhile subscription, but you can also use the free platform for many of your Treasure Legacy Collection projects.

Use Canva Pro to tell your stories in a quick, easy, and enjoyable format. Create Canva Pro presentations with photos you upload. If you upgrade to Canva Pro, it is about $13 monthly, and you can cancel when your Canva TLC project is complete. You can create collages, slideshows, and more and then easily share them with others.

Make unique, fun, and treasured greeting cards. We uploaded old, digitized photos to Canva Pro and made collages with fun graphics and fonts with those digitized old photos. The Canva photo collage you create can then be uploaded to a **photo printing website such as Shutterfly or Snapfish**. Many photo printing websites are available, so search online for which ones suit you best. The print quality of each company varies, so test print a few different companies and find the one or two companies you like best.

We have used the Canva-created photo collages to make the best birthday cards and "just for fun" cards to say hello, sending a printed picture to share. These greeting cards become a part of our TLC and can even include a piece of family history with Canva-typed text. Our coaching options shown at the end of this book can assist you with some of these projects.

UNLEASH THE FUN WITH CUSTOMIZED "ANY MILESTONE" ANNOUNCEMENT CARDS!

We have found that announcement cards are a great way to celebrate milestones in life and you can make them for any milestone, not just typical milestones such as graduations, weddings, and babies. We like to use announcement cards for anything we want to remember, and we can keep them just for our family history or share them with others.

If you look up synonyms for the word "milestone," you will find words like achievement, breakthrough, indicator, innovation, and groundbreaking. **For what moments in your life, and others' lives can you make a "milestone announcement card?"** It's simple and it creates joy, plus documents unique history as part of your TLC. We use Canva and Snapfish and you can search online to find your favorite ways to create milestone announcement cards.

In addition, custom greeting cards and Christmas ornaments are a great way to share photos and keep memories alive without creating a lot of "stuff and piles" to store over the years; even though ornaments are small gifts, they are meaningful.

USE YOUR SMARTPHONE TO DIGITIZE OLD PICTURES.

For old photos, you can use a *"smartphone transfer"* technique that may seem complicated at first, but it is actually quite easy, especially for those of us who remember the difficulties and expense of the days when we had to buy camera film, take a limited number of pictures on the film, and then get the film developed only to see how terrible the photos turned out!

Every smartphone today has a great camera; enjoy it! Take advantage of technology and transform your old photos into digital photocopies by taking a picture of them with your smartphone. You can learn to use your smartphone camera, including the editing features. If you need help, stop by your local smartphone store, and ask for assistance, take a workshop, or look online for "how to" videos.

Practice with the focus and alignment of the camera so you get a clear, balanced, digital photo of the old print photo. To me, this is a given, but it always surprises me when I ask someone to take a picture of an old print photo, and the digital copy they take with their camera is out of focus and has a weird angle. You can improve your skill at this with just a few tries. When your technique is perfected, you can get great-looking digital copies of old print photos that are preserved and protected for the ages, and they will be easy to share one-to-one or one-to-many in a group chat.

Go through old, printed photos, take pictures of them with your smartphone camera, and then text them out to loved ones so they can each have a digital copy. If you have social media accounts, you could upload the digitized copies there if that is easier.

The digitization and Canva creation process I use goes like this:

1) *Smartphone to Smartphone:* Take a picture of an old photo and send it to your loved ones on their smartphone so they have a copy to enjoy.

2) *Smartphone to Email:* Send the photo from your smartphone to your email. This may take some training and assistance; ask for help if you need it.

3) *Email to Computer:* Once the photo(s) are in your email, then download the photo(s) to your computer.

4) *Device to Canva:* **Get used to the term "device"** as it references any tech used such as computer, laptop, smartphone, or tablet. Many prefer one device over another and new ways of using these devices are always evolving, so get used to the word "device" meaning a computer, laptop, smartphone, tablet, and so forth. In Canva, you can easily upload a digital copy of the old photo(s) to use in collages, presentations, videos, greeting cards, and lots of other fun projects that are easy to create using text, headlines, images, fonts, colors, and more. Get help if you need it.

5) *Canva to Share with Others:* To share your Canva creations so others have them to enjoy, you can easily download your completed presentation, slideshow, story, videos, collage, et cetera, onto your computer and then send it to others through email for them to enjoy or you can use a platform such as Dropbox, One Drive, Google, or iCloud. You can also download your creations to a thumb drive or another external hard drive or upload them to a cloud storage service. If you need help with this, you can have a tech team such as Best Buy Geek Squad download your Canva creations onto an external drive for you.

6) *Device to Print Companies:* You can online search print companies such as Snapfish, Costco Photo, and Minted to look at their product options such as greeting cards, announcement cards, and even Christmas ornaments. These companies will have their own products and templates to shop through and you can upload your creations and digitized photos from your device.

Watch Canva Pro "how to" videos to learn the features, benefits, and how to complete tasks. Use their support as you explore their platform. Much of Canva Pro is intuitive and user-friendly, and I picked it up without any training. Keep your Canva login information written down in your TLC Journal/Binder so others can access your Canva account if needed.

You can search for "how to" videos and information from Google and YouTube. Canva also has a helpline. Best Buy, your local smartphone store clerks, and other local professionals can help. You can also invite your loved ones to help you create in Canva, which can be a memorable time together.

Warning: Canva can be addicting! When I discovered how easy and fun it was, I spent hours on Canva, creating all kinds of fun things. If you have younger kids in the family, it is nice to have a Canva project to learn together. It's very user-friendly and if you learn with a buddy, it can be twice as fun. I heard recently that the average person watches at least three hours of TV a day. We see this as an opportunity to switch some of that TV time to Canva time.

Note: Becoming more proficient in using technology comes with learning the ever-changing vocabulary terms in order to properly communicate with others. I am learning new terms every day such as "tech stack" which refers to what technology devices and platforms are being used to accomplish certain goals.

GET TO KNOW YOUR "TECH STACK" FOR YOUR TLC!

It's easy to put this off and say, "Someday," and then never do it and possibly regret it later. You can be intentional and block out a day, a weekend, a week, or whatever amount of time you want to allot, with or without the help of a loved one. We tackled many steps in our TLC by setting aside a day here, a weekend there, and a total of six weeks over the course of a year.

Our low-cost monthly subscription service and our one-on-one 90-day Coaching Programs can help you be intentional and accomplish your goals. Go to ForParents.EarthAdventuresForKids.com and scroll down to read about our coaching options.

You may have a learning curve ahead, but the payoff is creating and preserving wonderful memories and stories in an enjoyable format for you and your loved ones. Just as I experienced improvements in other parts of my life due to exercising my brain and trying new fitness classes—you could also experience many benefits from exercising your brain and learning new skills in technology. Once you get the hang of it, I am sure you will use Canva as easily as Bob Ross uses his paint medium for beautiful creations on his TV Show, *The Joy of Painting*. And as Bob Ross says, "We don't make mistakes, just happy little accidents." Some of my best Canva Pro work has been the result of my "happy little accidents."

Create powerful statements with the stories you want to share. Extract meaning from your major life experiences and accomplishments. Communicate your stories and history in typed words, images, videos, graphics, and formats with Canva Pro. You can use our books to write your TLC Legacy Lists to use as the basis for your stories and history. **In addition, add your own stories to your 5 TLC Legacy Lists with the following information:**

1. Who

2. What

3. Where

4. When

5. Why

6. What I've learned—a quick lesson of wisdom

Once you master the easy-to-use Canva platform as a way of telling your stories and using Canva to help capture your essence, energy, being, and mojo, you can download your Canva creations, share them, and preserve them on an external hard drive and/or in the cloud. You can keep copies in your TLC Save Forever Box and include written locations of the different storage places, such as the cloud or a thumb drive.

KEEP IT SIMPLE.

If telling your stories seems overwhelming, begin by creating an annual newsletter or photo collage with captions each winter season, focusing on one creation each year. Include pictures from the past twelve months or another time in your life/family life. Write short captions about the photos.

You can include a few interesting points from your past twelve months or other times in life, so those stories begin being told and written down for your family and others. In addition, this practice of reflecting back on a season to extract meaning helps us be intentional and look forward to the next season, setting goals and fulfilling our vision, taking the action steps that will get us where we want to go.

One year I made a collage for my mom with pictures of her and her siblings, two of whom have passed on. Now, each winter, as part of our TLC, this collage is a remembrance for my kids of their grandma and her siblings.

Another winter I created a photo book of a family trip we took to see my dad and I included old pictures from my dad's family and childhood. I digitized and uploaded old photos, so we had photos from current times and photos from 70-plus years ago when my dad, his siblings, and his parents were young. I was able to include some of the family history from my dad and now this history is preserved in a fun, enjoyable, easy-to-access format for future generations.

Note: Christmas and winter holidays can be a time when people challenge the celebrations and traditions, some saying, "That's a "Christian" thing or that's a "pagan" thing. We have done our research, and we see it as a blend of origins, with roots in what we see as a time of dark, cold, and challenging winter—and for thousands of years, people have made the best of it. They come together in a giving spirit and make merry in as many ways as they can. There was a time when I did not celebrate anything in winter, and now, I celebrate from Thanksgiving to the New Year! I am fascinated by the multi-cultural celebrations and thankful for many traditions handed down from the ages in a spirit of goodwill, sending us good tidings. I think it is a matter of the heart and joy to the world. You decide what works for you.

Other tech options to consider:

You can go to companies such as www.LegacyBox.com to learn about their service for digitizing and protecting your past VHS tapes, videos, films, photos, and audio recordings. Compare this to using Best Buy or Staples services or other transfer services. We bought a device from Costco years ago to transfer our old VHS tapes onto DVD. Now we are ready to transfer those DVDs to an external hard drive. Sometimes it is easier to pay for a professional service.

Make sure to take precautions with backups and take other protective measures. Decide if you want to send your non-replaceable, treasured keepsakes through a mail service. Maybe finding a local professional is a better option for you. Whatever you decide, take steps to preserve and protect your photos and videos, getting them into formats in which you and others can enjoy and extract meaning and value from your life's experiences.

We enjoy watching *My Legacy List* **on PBS** and you can watch it to see the processes they go through, helping people find their treasures and tell their stories. You can online search for other movies, documentaries, and TV shows on organizing, creating legacies, and so forth so that you can mentally prepare for the process seeing the beginning, the middle, and the end result—also learning the "why" for different people.

The "why" is very important to know because it will get you through all the phases of the process. Many times, there is some sort of "pain point" involved for the person or others. It is common to hear, "Do you want the pain of staying the same or the pain of change?" The pain of change will bring rewards, what does the pain of staying the same bring? We have discussed earlier in this book exploring the question, "What happens if I do nothing and do not create my TLC?" This will be for you and those involved to answer.

Tell your stories with our books as your how-to guide.

Our books are the guide and road map of how we navigated the journey of raising kids, caring for others, and moving through changing seasons and phases of life with grace. In our Journal Stories on our Journal page at www.EarthAdventuresForKids.com we show you how we used the tools during times of:

- Chaos

- Demanding schedules

- Seasonal and long-term stress
- Fast-paced, busy lifestyles
- Unexpected challenges and emergencies
- Budget shortfalls

OUR TOOLS MADE US WILDLY SUCCESSFUL, AND IN OUR BOOKS, WE SHOW YOU HOW WE DID IT!

Was it always easy? No. Were we perfect? No. Did we make mistakes? Yes. Overall, we made it through the peaks and valleys, the obstacles, the pitfalls, the sinking sand, and all the other types of testing that come against "smooth sailing" in life. Our books also show you how to "pass the torch" to others so they can carry on, teaching the next generations.

You, too, have wisdom, experience, and information you need to pass on to others. We help you get:

- ★ your stories
- ★ your TLC—tender, loving, care and
- ★ your practical steps of instruction and valued information

into your own formats for you to pass on to others as part of your legacy with improved relationships and communication. Whether you're thinking of your kids, loved ones, or the community, you will want to pass on your best information from your life well-lived.

Comprehensive and complete, our books show you how to get the best information from your life into easy-to-access, enjoyable formats to benefit yourself and others. You can do it yourself using our books as your guide or sign up for our coaching programs for extra help.

You might only need help in certain areas of life as you might already be "smooth sailing" in other areas. Our quizzes help you determine whether your status quo in certain areas is working for you or not. Download our free quiz at ForParents.EarthAdventuresForKids.com and opt-in to join our community to stay updated about events, special offers, and new releases.

OUR BOOKS AND TOOLS HELP YOU DEFINE YOUR CLASSIC.

Stedman Graham, author of *Identity Leadership: To Lead Others You Must First Lead Yourself,* declares on his website at https://stedmangraham.com/ the following: ". . . Identity Leadership, which is self-leadership based on the philosophy that you cannot lead anyone until you first lead yourself. . . 'leadership is everything.'"

At Grant Cardone's Growth Con 2022, Stedman Graham stated that you have to know who you are and then organize and make it relevant to your heart and mind. Develop a vision for your life and seasons and then create a roadmap plan to reach your goals—our books and tools show you how.

You are unique, and you have a life story—a signature talk—as speaking coach Pete Vargas calls it. Learn how one signature talk changed his life for the better by improving his relationship with his dad. You can read his story at Advance Your Reach https://advanceyourreach.com/about/.

Our books, tools, and coaching help you:

★ Define your classic.

★ Develop your stories.

★ Tell your stories in a variety of formats that make it easy for you and others to access and enjoy.

Stories change lives. And as Chandler Bolt of SelfPublishing.com says, "Books change lives." He goes on to say that books not only change the lives of the readers but also of the authors. Our books and tools help you write your stories and preserve and share the best information about your life well-lived, which can change your life and other's lives for the better.

MANY PEOPLE SAY, "I WANT TO WRITE A BOOK," BUT THEY NEVER START, OR THEY NEVER FINISH.

Our proven methods and formats, as outlined in our books and coaching, help you start and finish that book or guide you are ready to write. Easy, manageable steps are outlined, and we have proven processes to help you unleash the power of your personal storytelling. For example, many of our books prompt you to write your own lists. These lists are the foundation for your "classic" unique stories.

In our coaching programs, we help you get your stories written, in a preserved and easy-to-access format for your legacy, and if you like, we help you get them ready for you to submit your work to professional editors, proofreaders, and a publisher.

Whether your stories and the best information from your life well-lived are for your family, loved ones, community, or business—whatever your sphere of influence—we can help you get organized, write your outline, develop your stories, and get them preserved and shared in formats that are easy-to-access and enjoyable. Read our books for all the steps and sign up for our coaching programs! You can also give our books and coaching as gifts to others.

How can writing down your stories improve your life and others' lives? Telling your stories of your life well-lived helps improve your life and others' lives by:

★ Affirming your learned wisdom.

★ Affirming your values and pillars.

★ Showing practical ways to apply timeless principles for great outcomes.

★ Giving "the moral of the story" insights that can help others avoid pitfalls in life.

★ Providing entertainment, humor, laughter, and inspiration as you might want to tell stories of adventure and unexpected outcomes with elements of surprise.

★ Providing a sense of worthiness in life including enduring the trials that can come with it.

★ Developing your own mindset of seeing the best in the worst as you might want to tell stories of adversity and overcoming challenges.

★ Preserving valuable history and knowledge.

WE HAVE THE PROVEN METHODS AND FORMATS TO HELP YOU WRITE YOUR STORIES.

We look forward to helping you write your 5 TLC Legacy Lists, focus your ideas, get your outline, develop your points and highlights, conclude the stories, and get them into easy-to-access and enjoyable formats of your choice. Are you interested in getting them published professionally? We can help direct you there too.

Note: In addition to our coaching costs, there are additional costs associated with getting the stories into formats of your choice, depending on how you choose to proceed. Most costs are minimal if you are just using them for personal legacy purposes, as opposed to using them for business and professional use.

For more information, visit us at ForParents.EarthAdventuresForKids.com and scroll down to the coaching section.

CHAPTER 8

GET YOUR TLC SAVE FOREVER BOXES, TLC JOURNAL/BINDERS AND CATCH-ALL BAGS

First, let's recap. Getting familiar with each tool in the Treasure Legacy Collection will help you get more value from it. The more you utilize and become familiar with each tool and start using the tools in your days and nights, the more you will see new applications and crossover of where different tools can be applied to different situations, thereby extracting even more value and meaning from your TLC tools and system.

Inform your loved ones about the TLC Method, including the books and tools and how you use them. Bring your loved ones into your Treasure Legacy Collection creation and enjoyment. Be prepared, when you first inform them, it might not be a good time for them to get involved as they may be busy with their own objectives in life, so don't take it personally if they need to decline the invitation at the moment. You can invite them again and again with no pressure. Going solo in creating your TLC is a great option with many rewards and you will likely meet others along the journey of creating your TLC.

Join our email list at www.EarthAdventuresForKids.com to be notified of our community events and new releases. There are many of us "going solo" in creating our TLC and we have formed our own community. Going solo is a foundation of the Earth Adventures For Kids lifestyle. We forge our own path!

You can suggest to others that they create their own TLC at the same time you create your TLC so you can share experiences and assist each other by sharing information, resources, and general support. You could also find an accountability partner to help you commit to a section of creating your TLC, finish it, and then commit to another section. The entire TLC process can be done in one to twelve months, depending on your pace. This is another example of living the TLC lifestyle—you just incorporate what you can in a given season and make it a regular part of life. You can make "adding in a new section of your TLC each season" a part of your lifestyle.

We offer a low-cost monthly subscription service and one-on-one 90-day Coaching Programs if you would like our assistance. We will add webinar group coaching options too. For more information on our coaching, go to ForParents.EarthAdventuresForKids.com and scroll down to the coaching section.

Read this book in its entirety and read through the bullet point lists, checklists, quizzes, and worksheets in this book. Become familiar with the processes outlined. Take inventory of your situation, items, and tasks at hand, "sizing up" the process, and estimating time and assistance requirements. From the digital copies of our books, print the quizzes, checklists, bullet point lists, and worksheets and keep them on a clipboard for quick reference of what you need to do and where you are in the process of creating your TLC.

DO YOU HAVE A LOT OF STUFF-AND-PILES-TO-SORT-AND-DECIDE-THROUGH?

Plan the work in stages. Don't get overwhelmed, as you can break down the components of the TLC and complete one item each week or complete one section each month or season until all points are completed. Outsourcing some parts of the process can help speed things up and reduce the overwhelm. It is helpful to plan the portions of the process that you will outsource to others. For example, you might want to pay for assistance with more challenging parts and you may need to budget for the extra cost.

The items in the TLC and the steps involved in creating your TLC are talking points for conversations that may otherwise be difficult to start. Are there topics you don't know how to discuss with your loved ones? Use the TLC as your guide.

Note: Make sure trusted, loved ones are informed of 1) how to access and 2) how to use your TLC in your absence, no matter what phase of creating your TLC you are in.

What is your unique take on all the components of the Treasure Legacy Collection using your tender, loving, care and wishes for your loved ones? **Determine what is most important to you and include it in your TLC.** Keep things simple.

You might want to expand more on one aspect of your TLC and do less in another area. You may choose to skip some areas. After you become familiar with each tool and the system, decide where you want to start. You can quickly get through each item and then, later, go back to each component and add in more details.

★ Begin your process by **buying our labels for your TLC Save Forever Box(es) and TLC Journal/Binder(s)** so you can properly label your TLC and easily identify and communicate to others that these containers and binders are part of your TLC.

★ **After you buy your labels, source the TLC Save Forever Box containers and TLC Journal/Binders** you want to use. Ensure the label adhesive will stick adequately to the container and Journal/Binder you choose.

FOR THE TLC SAVE FOREVER BOX, we like to use clear plastic, stackable matching boxes, about the size of 22" x 11" so they are not too heavy and are easy to manage. You can see our TLC Save Forever Boxes and TLC Journal/Binders on our website at www.EarthAdventuresForKids.com under the Shop section.

We have sourced our containers at places like Costco, Staples, Target, Home Depot, World Market, and Bed Bath & Beyond. Again, ensure our TLC Save Forever Box label adhesive will stick to your container(s). Every winter, Costco usually has a great price on clear, stackable, matching containers. I try to buy these when they have them at Costco due to the great price.

Note: For managing the incoming, outgoing, and storage of items in a space, you can choose different types of containers that fit your décor and your budget. If containers or journal/binders are not specifically part of your TLC, or your Signature Collection as discussed in our book *How to Create Your Own Signature Collection*, and they are just for managing incoming, outgoing, and storage of items, then they do not need our labels—so the containers and journal/binders can be made of different materials that don't need to allow the stickiness of our labels.

THE TLC JOURNAL/BINDER can be as simple as a hardcover, three-inch ring binder about 10 ½" x 11 ½" in size, that has a clear plastic sleeve already attached on the front and back, which is handy for sliding a title page or other papers into the front and back outside cover. We usually get ours from Staples, Target, or a similar store.

We also recommend buying clear protective sleeves that can be added to the three-ring binder to insert papers, writings, documents, memorabilia, and so on. We like the protective sleeve that can handle multiple items and can be added as one inclusion on the rings. We also add a series of **pocket folders** into the three-ring binder to insert multiple items, such as important papers, documents, writings, and so on, as one inclusion into the rings. This makes it easy to store and protect many items in an organized and easy-to-flip-through format that is easy to find, identify, and communicate to others that it is part of your TLC.

THE KEY WORD IS "EASY."

You may have things easy for you, but we are making them easy for others as well,

as it will be your loved ones who will appreciate your TLC and its ease of use.

You may want multiple TLC Journal/Binders depending on how much you include. Buy our label for each TLC Journal/Binder you have. I like keeping a binder for just my passwords and login info. Most accounts now are associated with email addresses and phone numbers for verification and resetting passwords, so make sure to have this info associated with each account safely stored in your TLC Journal/Binder with corresponding account info in case your trusted loved ones need to access the information in the event of an emergency.

Keeping a separate binder for account info is much easier to access and use when needed, as my TLC Journal/Binders are often full of different types of items and are not accessed as often. I also have a separate financial TLC Journal/Binder just for asset information. These should each have your TLC Journal/Binder Label affixed to them for easy communication to others that it is part of your TLC.

For example, my TLC Journal/Binder is a set of three binders and one clipboard. You can use this easy reference list to help you complete your TLC Jounral/Binder set:

★ **Binder 1** includes small memorabilia, wisdom writings, and so on.

★ **Binder 2** is for account info, passwords, and login information.

★ **Binder 3** is for assets including important keys. I can store the keys in the binder because I add in the clear sleeve protectors that will also hold sets of keys in addition to other important documents.

★ **Clipboard** - I keep my Financial Worksheet on a clipboard in my daily desk routine, as I use it Monday through Friday to assess my financial position, balance my accounts, manage cash flow, bill pay, et cetera.

GET YOUR CATCH-ALL BAGS.

A Catch-All Bag can be any reusable, free-standing bag and we prefer our large bags to be at least 18.65" tall x 18.65" long x 5.92" interior width. Our favorite large bags are washable and made of 100 percent polypropylene, able to carry 26.45 pounds, cost about $2 at many stores, and are easy to fold down and pack into smaller spaces.

I like the festive, seasonal bags from Bed Bath & Beyond and other businesses like TJ Maxx, Marshalls, and World Market that are often at check-out and usually cost about $2 each. Costco, from time to time, has nice, insulated "grocery" bags that I buy if I like the style. Costco had some fun Hawaiian print bags for $5 years ago, and I used them as Catch-All Bags for everything except groceries! More recently, Costco had some great free-standing insulated bags for about $9 that were made of woven linen-like material.

The bags should be able to "free-stand" independently—a great feature for easily putting items in and taking them out. Whole Foods and other grocery stores often have free-standing reusable bags in fun, seasonal designs. We use them for everything but groceries! Free-standing Catch-All Bags allow us to easily view contents stored inside the bag, sort, store, organize, take on the go, keep the car organized, separate different activities and projects, and so forth.

To be versatile and ready for action with your Catch-All Bags, think of "nesting dolls" and how smaller dolls fit inside larger ones. We do this nesting with our Catch-All Bags. To get organized with nesting bags, we use the mini Catch-All Bag and we use various sizes of Ziploc baggies within purses, backpacks, and larger Catch-All Bags. The various sizes of Ziploc bags allow you to have a lot of stuff, but rather than having a bunch of loose items, they are separated into different Ziploc baggies, which makes items easy to access, easy to rummage through, and items are protected inside a Ziploc baggie.

Use the "nesting bags" concept to make your days and nights better by being organized, versatile, quick in responses, flexible, ready to go, and able to handle many situations with your system of "nesting bags" using different sizes of Catch-All bags, various sizes of Ziploc bags, Parker Clay bags/ purses, and other bags you find work for you. This helps you keep separate categories and keep like-items together with protection of the items making them easy to find, access, use, and so forth instead of spending valuable time rummaging through loose items.

THE CATCH-ALL BAG MAGIC IN ACTION . . .

The free-standing feature of The Catch-All Bag allows QUICK

1) access to adding items in the bag.

2) assessment of what items are in the bag.

3) removal of items from the bag.

4) ability to nest smaller bags within larger bags.

Allowing you to sort and decide quickly, plus the "nesting of bags within bags" capability makes The Catch-All Bag one of our "must-haves" in our organization system for improving quality of life. Time is key when I am quickly packing or unpacking because every minute counts when you have a timeline to stay on and demands to keep up with.

Rareform is a bag company that repurposes old billboards into beautiful bags. I joined their email list to get notified of new releases and special offers. Check them out at https://www.rareform. com/ and I am sure you will be amazed at how they change old billboards into usable bags. We also love **Parker Clay** leather bags, and we love their purpose. You can learn more here https://www. parkerclay.com/pages/impact and make sure to join their email list.

KEEP IT ALL TOGETHER WITH THE CATCH-ALL BAG.

The key feature in a Catch-All Bag is that it is **free-standing** meaning the bag will stand upright on its own. The free-standing feature enables you to quickly see what is in the bag, quickly add to the contents, and quickly remove the contents as needed. When life is busy and demanding, having these features in your organization system will make a huge difference in being able to accomplish your objectives, complete tasks, handle responsibilities, and do it in a fun, festive way that makes it **look like you "have it all together" because you do!**

We will post videos on our website demonstrating our tools, techniques, and the materials we use, so be sure to join our email list to be notified of updates, events, and new releases. We will also host webinars for low-cost group coaching; join our email list to get notified of these opportunities.

After sourcing your TLC Save Forever Boxes, your TLC Journal/Binders, and your Catch-All Bags, you will be ready to begin placing items into these containers, which means it is time to take on the "sort and decide through the stuff and piles" phase.

CHAPTER 9

TLC HOME CLEANING AND ORGANIZATION

Here we go with the often-unpopular topic of home cleaning and organization. **But do not worry! We have helpful strategies to make it easy!** We all accumulate stuff. Some will have more, some less and this could depend on how many times you have moved in the last decade or two. I found it easier to tackle this task for my mom and go through her stuff rather than for me to go through my own stuff. If you can recruit someone to help you or hire someone to assist in some parts of the process, it might be easier. Sometimes having a non-attached person assisting you will help you move through the process of sorting and decision-making. This person acts as a coach to help you move through the process, offering support when you get stuck and motivating you to move through the whole, occasionally difficult, process.

WE CALL THIS PHASE OF HOME ORGANIZATION THE "SORT AND DECIDE THRU THE STUFF AND PILES" PHASE.

Being able to know where you are in the process and phases can help you stay motivated and keep moving forward to your goal. If you are ready to tackle the "sort and decide through the stuff and piles" phase, it helps to plan the work with a strategy and the right mindset. If you have a copy of our digital book, you can **print the many checklists and bullet point lists we have throughout this book and put them on a clipboard** to refer to them through this phase and help you if you get stuck in the process somewhere. Just read through the lists and see what information helps you keep moving forward.

After being in the same home for seventeen years, I have gone through our stuff about ten times thoroughly, and I must say, each time, it was terrible. It is not always easy, and I had an organized home! It's the closets, the drawers, the cabinets, the garage, those places where things get hidden away, out of sight, out of mind. It is the sorting and decision-making in those spaces that is overwhelming.

Keep a governing mindset of the benefits of going through every closet, drawer, cabinet, and so on. Ask yourself if you want 1) the pain of staying the same or 2) the pain of change which leads to rewards. Doing the hard work will lead to these rewards:

★ Creating a new look in the room and space.

★ Allowing others to benefit from the stuff you give away or sell.

★ Having new ways to use the space.

★ Finding, enjoying, and preserving your most treasured items.

★ Being more efficient in an organized space.

★ Getting the results you really want in life.

Identify the most relevant benefits of **WHY** you are going through all your stuff and keep those benefits as a guiding mindset you repeat to yourself and to others as you go through the process. Expect the middle of the process to be chaotic to a degree, depending on how much is in your "stuff and piles." Manage through it and keep going, sorting one item at a time, deciding to 1) keep, 2) toss or recycle, 3) sell or 4) give away.

If there is a "bunch of stuff" in one space such as a drawer, closet, or room, you can choose to dump it all out at one time and just place back in the items you know you want and need in that space. This is much faster and easier than sorting items one by one. You will need containers on hand to "dump a bunch of stuff into" all at once. These containers can be Catch-All Bags, clean trash bags, clear plastic containers, or cardboard boxes. If the job is large enough, the container can even be a trailer in the driveway or a U-Haul truck to use as a sorting station outside of your home.

Here is my approach to organizing my home and office. First, decide how to organize the space in a new way and how you will handle the following categories for a specific space:

1) Incoming items

2) Outgoing items

3) Storage of items

These three categories can apply to home, office, finances, car, et cetera. For example, the home has incoming items from people who live in your household. Someone might bring home art they made, gifts a friend gave them, stuff they bought, and so on. How will you handle the incoming? **Read our book, *How to Create Your Own Signature Collection,* to help with this system.**

EXAMPLES OF INCOMING ITEMS are in the specific space of finances. You
have incoming bills, streams of income, and incoming demands on your budget. How do you handle the incoming items in your finances? Read our book, *How to Create a Financial Worksheet,* to get organized with these incoming items.

EXAMPLES OF OUTGOING ITEMS are in the specific spaces of the office and
the car. Think of all the things you need to file-away-off-your-desk or take out to the car and drop off in errands. Anything that needs to move out of a specific space into another is considered outgoing. Different sizes of Catch-All Bags with "nesting options" are great for handling these items that deal with running errands and bringing stuff in and out of the car as needed. One nesting option I love is when I put my purse—which is usually a free-standing bag from Parker Clay—in a large Catch-All Bag and then add all my errand items into the same Catch-All Bag to take out to the car as one item. **Note:** About every 5-7 years, I go through my files and purge and refresh them as a way to keep the physical storage of documents under control, up to date, and relevant.

EXAMPLES OF STORAGE OF ITEMS deal with containers of all different types. Where can you use our Save Forever Box container that is talked about in our Signature Collection book? Where can you use our TLC Save Forever Box container? Where can you use our Catch-All Bags as containers? Where do you need our labels for identifying what is in containers? You can buy different containers that are in the form of storage cabinets, shelves, bins, boxes, bags et cetera. Get ideas from catalogs, online sites, and stores like Pottery Barn, California Closets, Restoration Hardware, Target, Home Depot, and IKEA.

Having "places in the spaces" is essential! This means having places—also known as containers—to put items in that are in the space you are deciding to organize. Whether it is a room in the house, the desk paperwork, the car with incoming and outgoing items, or whatever, you need to first decide how you will handle the incoming, outgoing, and storage of items that may now be in a clutter of "stuff and piles."

Having "places for the spaces" means having containers to place things in. The containers are the places you will be sorting into such as having a box or clean trash bag for all the giveaway stuff and containers that fit your décor for all the storage of the stuff you will keep. Decide how you want to store the items you will keep in that space—maybe you will choose a cubicle wall unit as seen in many storage solutions at IKEA, Pottery Barn, and California Closets.

Look online, in magazines, or in catalogs to get ideas of what organized spaces with great storage solutions look like and decide what you want in your specific spaces. **Decide what types of bins, containers, baskets, bags, plastic baggies, files, binders, and shelving units you like,** and determine your budget.

You can look at places like California Closets, IKEA, Target, Costco, World Market, Staples, Pottery Barn, Crate and Barrel, The Container Store, and so forth for inspiration and then set out to find what you need at a price that works for you. Also, check out the website for California Closets https://www.californiaclosets.com/ to see how they handle a variety of spaces. Go to our website to see our videos and images of different "places for the spaces" and join our email list to get updates on our events, new releases, and special offers. After you have the containers—the places for the spaces—the next phase of work will be all about "sorting and decision-making."

"STUFF AND PILES" MEET "BAGS IN BAGS."

Before we take on the "sorting and decision-making" process, be aware of another successful way we deal with "stuff and piles" clutter that accumulates not only in rooms, cars, garages, drawers, closets, and even purses. Our success in being clutter-free is with the "**bags in bags**" concept, also known as "nesting bags." As part of nesting bags within bags, I learned to use different sizes of Ziploc clear plastic baggies as one way of organizing spaces.

For example, I will add my hair ties, bobby pins, small brush, et cetera, into a quart-size plastic Ziploc and keep it in a drawer, in my purse, or in a Catch-All Bag so I can rummage through the contents of the space easily. Instead of having a bunch of loose items, I will instead have different-sized, clear, plastic Ziploc baggies with many items grouped together in one bag.

Rummaging through items that are in clear, plastic baggies is easier and faster than wasting time rummaging through all loose items. The clear plastic allows me to easily see what is in that baggie and only pull the baggie I need at the moment. It's a great technique to use in purses, baskets, bins, and drawers.

For example, in a drawer, you can have a plastic Ziploc baggie to store items like nail clippers, tweezers, and nail files all in one plastic baggie. And in the console of my car, I like to keep a clear, plastic Ziploc baggie of items I may need on the go, like small moisturizer bottles, antiseptic, lip balm, deodorant, toothbrush and toothpaste, floss, et cetera.

The "bags in bags" or "nesting bags" concept allows you to be versatile and ready for many situations at a moment's notice. For example, you can put smaller-sized, mini Catch-All Bags in the larger Catch-All Bags, nesting them with smaller bags in larger bags. I have a few different larger purses that are beautiful from Parker Clay www.ParkerClay.com and I like to change purses depending on what I am doing. I have found that keeping my wallet and other regular must-haves in a foldable, mini Catch-All Bag about 8"x 10" inside my Parker Clay bag allows me to change purses easily. I simply take the mini Catch-All Bag out of one purse and put it in another, this way I am sure I have all my necessities with me no matter which purse I am using. I have my other purse items, such as makeup, in various sizes of clear plastic Ziploc baggies so if I need to grab other items quickly, I can easily do so, and keep everything I need with me, no matter which purse I am using.

Depending on the outing I am going on, I will even add my Parker Clay purse/bag into the larger Catch-All Bag so I will have more nesting bags. If I run a quick errand, I can pull out my Parker Clay bag and run into the store, leaving the Catch-All Bag with other items stored in the car.

The perfect mini Catch-All Bags can be found at Lululemon (the free bag at checkout), World Market (low-cost bags at check out), grocery stores, and so forth. **Any reusable bag that is free-standing and smaller in size will work for nesting smaller bags within larger bags**. This makes you more organized and ready for a variety of situations. Various sizes of Ziploc bags can be used to store items in your purse, so you do not have to rummage through your purse looking through loose items. I have many memories as a child waiting for my mom to find her keys or something else in all her loose items in her purse. With the use of the nesting, bags-in-bags concept, you don't have to do this! Different sizes of Ziploc baggies are great for organizing!

Go to our website at www.EarthAdventuresForKids.com to join our email list so you will be notified when we post demonstration videos of us using the nesting, bags-in-bags concepts.

DEALING WITH "STUFF AND PILES" IS PART OF LIFE.

Getting organized is mostly about SORTING items and DECIDING what to do with it all. This can be exhausting, overwhelming, and often seems endless. Take heart and be encouraged; you are not alone. **We all have to deal with stuff and piles,** consider it part of the human experience.

The "Sorting and Deciding of the Stuff and Piles" Process

The "sorting and deciding of the stuff and piles" process can be the least desirable, but the most rewarding in all the phases of organizing. The trick is to maintain a steady forward momentum even though it may feel like you are walking through endless obstacles with no light at the end of the tunnel. If this is the case, to get through it, I will go into hyper-drive with a clear vision of the end result I want and just power through faster in the sorting and deciding actions. It can become like a game of quick decisions.

Our "stuff and piles" vary, depending on what is happening and what has happened in our lives in a particular season. And oftentimes, we have a backlog of stuff and piles because life came at us so fast; so many events and activities occurred in the same season we could not keep up or did not want to keep up because we were accomplishing other priorities at the time.

Evaluate items in a particular space and how they currently exist in the "space" of a room, a cabinet, a drawer, a purse, a closet, a car, or a storage container. Do items in a space appear to be in piles everywhere? This is what we call, "stuff and piles." Some piles can be a foot high, some even higher than that. If you have "stuff and piles," assess the size and the strategy for dealing with it.

As kids, when told to clean our room, we would "bulldoze sweep" everything on the floor into our closet and shut the door. We would yell, "Don't open that door!" if anyone went near the closet as the pile was about 3 feet high in the closet! No kidding! Our strategy for dealing with our "stuff and piles" was to make one huge pile of stuff from the smaller piles of stuff.

You can work to develop this skill of evaluating how items exist in a particular space. When you go places, notice how stores and other people keep their stuff. Take notice of what you like and what you want for your space.

ASK YOURSELF THE FOLLOWING QUESTIONS FOR YOUR SPACE:

★ How can I apply the TLC Method of Mindset, Tools, Systems, and Marketplace in this space and situation?

★ Can the space be reorganized?

★ Do I like the way this room looks and feels? Do I like how it handles the incoming, outgoing, and storage of items? Is the current system helping or hindering me and others?

★ How will this space handle incoming, outgoing, and storage items after I am done organizing?

★ Can I use matching or complementary storage bins that are decorative, clear, and stackable?

★ Can I use decorative storage cabinets that are closed-door or open storage with a cube/cubby style?

★ Is the stuff necessary, accessible, and easily identified for what it is?

★ Does this room present a problem(s)? Or is this room a joy?

★ Can I use different sizes of free-standing Catch-All Bags to help handle incoming, outgoing, and storage of items to help with being ready for many situations?

★ Do I need festive, fun Catch-All Bags to separate projects and categories so that instead of random, cluttered "stuff and piles" of items, items are instead organized by project, activity, or grouped with similar items in separate, festive, fun Catch-All Bags?

★ Can I use the nesting "bags in bags" concept with different sizes of clear plastic baggies and Catch-All Bags to put items in, and make things easier to see, keeping them separate for when I need to easily access them?

Get organizing tips online by looking at stores such as IKEA, Pottery Barn, Restoration Hardware, The Container Store, California Closets, and World Market Cost Plus. Search online for storage bins and storage cabinets. Find storage containers that speak to you and how you would like to have your rooms look.

Use our labels to mark your TLC Save Forever Box(es) and TLC Journal/Binders. You will want to read about our Save Forever Box in our book, *How to Create Your Own Signature Collection*, as this book discusses using our tools to create your own systems of dealing with incoming, outgoing, and storage of items in all types of spaces. You can look at our website at www.EarthAdventuresForKids. com to see the TLC Save Forever Box, Save Forever Box images, Label images, and Catch-All Bag images in action.

We will post videos demonstrating the use of our tools on our website at www. EarthAdventuresForKids.com so visit us at our website and join our email list to receive notifications of updates, new releases, and more. Sign up for our low-cost monthly subscription or our one-on-one coaching programs to get our assistance moving you through the process of "sorting and deciding through the stuff and piles" phase.

OPTIONS FOR GETTING THROUGH THE "SORTING AND DECIDING THRU STUFF AND PILES" PROCESS:

★ Sometimes hiring a professional organizer to help complete a task or two is necessary or desired — or get a friend or family member to help.

★ Sometimes it is necessary to "clean slate" a space by taking everything out of the space and then returning only what is desired or needed. We call this a **Clean-Slate-Dump-Into-a-Sorting-Container**. The "sorting containers" can be clean trash bags, Catch-All Bags, cardboard boxes, clear plastic containers, or even a trailer or U-Haul if the job is big enough. This "clean slate dump action" does not mean you are not protecting or valuing the items. Instead, you are using this as a "batching" technique that allows you to quickly empty a space.

Master the TLC Cleaning: The home cleaning and organizing part of the TLC-creating process can be lengthy, depending on how many times you have moved over the years and how you have kept the items in your house and garage. Use our checklists, bullet point lists, and worksheets to help you make it through. Print what you want to keep on a clipboard and reference the information throughout the process to keep you on track and moving forward. You might get stuck in some areas and the information on the clipboard can help you get unstuck.

Become good at sorting and use the following decision-making guides:

1) Keep for use.

2) Keep for enjoyment.

3) Keep for Treasure Legacy Collection, handing it down through generations.

4) Toss, trash, recycle.

5) Donate or give to others.

6) Sell.

A guiding principle in this process is that if you do not handle these items now, your loved ones will need to go through them in your absence, and they might not know the significance or stories behind the item. When you do the TLC cleaning, you help your loved ones appreciate and understand the meaning and significance of your treasures. You can take pictures of certain items and attach the story to the items. This can make it easier to let go of the physical item. Our coaching programs can help you write your stories and attach your photos to your stories. Go to ForParents. EarthAdventuresForKids.com and scroll to the coaching section to learn more.

VIRTUAL ASSISTANCE FOR YOUR TLC

Another use of modern technology is virtual assistance in TLC creation. Loved ones can take part in your TLC cleaning with you, even if they live in different regions, by using modern technology such as smartphones and tablets that offer the ability to take endless photos and make video calls. You can have a friend or relative, even a coach, on a Zoom call and go through the items together.

We offer a low-cost monthly subscription and one-on-one 90-day Coaching Programs if you would like assistance. Go to ForParents.EarthAdventuresForKids.com and scroll down to the coaching section to learn more. We will also host webinars for low-cost group coaching, so be sure to join our email list to get notified of these opportunities.

Use tact and care as you go through the TLC process with loved ones. We did the TLC cleaning process with one relative, and we realized she was keeping a lot of her mom's old makeup and accessories, thinking her mom would come back someday and use them. We helped her see the "reality" of what was happening—as her mom had passed on ten years before. The true reality was that the old products were a health hazard and needed to be tossed. The old products were cluttering up her counter space. We cleared out the space with the batch technique of a "clean slate dump" into clean grocery bags and took the bags out onto a nice table with chairs and helped sort item by item, and we took the time to hear the stories of the different old products that belonged to her mom. Afterward, she enjoyed a fresh look in the room with more usable counter space.

This example shows that many parts of the process of TLC cleaning and clearing out of the "stuff and piles" are also remembering loved ones who have passed on and recalling details of the past that may be difficult. Past moments may be re-lived, and with that may come an emotional response. Our strategies help you and your loved ones move through the process easier. Have a moment of silence to honor the past if needed but then keep moving forward.

KEEP THE MAIN THING THE MAIN THING AND MOVE ON THROUGH THE TOUGH STUFF!

When we have helped others do their TLC cleaning, and when we have done our own TLC cleaning, we have developed some helpful techniques for going through the emotional decision-making process on what to do with the items. Keep in mind that some emotions that come up with TLC cleaning can range from pleasant to difficult and encompass everything in between; however, keep moving forward. Pre-determine at the beginning of the "sorting-and-deciding-of-the-stuff-and-piles" process that you will power through the sorting and deciding phase to get to that very last item in the space.

Essential principles to keep in mind are:

1) Think of all that is gained from the TLC cleaning process.

2) Keep a vision for the "new space" and the "new way of life" created.

3) Maintain a focus on the items serving out their useful life; does the item need to go to another person who will use it, or does it need to go to recycling/trash to become something else? Keep in mind companies like Rareform https://www.rareform.com/ that are making old things new.

4) What is the pain of staying the same? What is the pain of change and the resulting rewards?

POINTS TO KEEP IN MIND AND KEEP YOU MOVING FORWARD:

✓ **Come to terms with aging products and old technology.** Sometimes, it is hard to accept that items have a useful life and occasionally must be recycled for parts or tossed. Keep in mind all the tech people searching for old technology to use for something. Trust that the items let go of will be turned into something new, and also appreciated and enjoyed by others.

✓ **Come to terms with the "money paid" for items in the past.** Always ask, "What am I missing out on because I have this "stuff and piles" clutter here?" A better use of space can be created when the clutter is gone, and your quality of life and relationships are improved.

✓ **TLC cleaning is about finding and sharing your treasures and creating enjoyable, functional, efficient spaces.** Organized spaces that function well add to the quality of life, improve relationships, and improve communication. When the clutter is gone, items are categorized, sorted, and stored in a beautiful way that facilitates an enjoyable environment.

This allows for new experiences and new memories. Look forward to a new way of life—you, but better!

✓ **Wear a mask and gloves.** We don't realize that dust collects, and we send it into our breathing space. I have had many times where I forgot to put on a mask and regretted it later. Gloves can help too. In some spaces, you don't know what you will find lurking, so take precautions.

✓ **Warning:** Clutters of "stuff and piles" become habitats for critters! This can be a motivating factor to keep spaces tidy and keep "stuff and piles" off the floor. My kids were always motivated to pick up stuff off the floor when I reminded them that spiders like dark places that they could hide in.

✓ **Hazardous materials need to be disposed of in the proper ways.** Check with your local garbage collection, dump, and with stores like Home Depot on their disposal abilities. Most pharmacies now carry postage-paid baggies that you can put old medications in and just drop the bag in the mail if it meets the requirements.

✓ **Look online to see what organizations and businesses will reuse and re-purpose** old arts and crafts items, old colored markers, and other types of items where crafty people can make good use of them. Look online to see if there are Maker Spaces in your area. https://www.makerspaces.com/what-is-a-makerspace/ You can join a Maker Space like this one https://www.slomakerspace.com/ and see the possibilities for turning the old into new.

✓ **Develop a plan and timeline of how to handle each space.** Ask loved ones if they can help one weekend or one week. Over one year, I helped my mom for a total of six weeks—one week at a time—and we mixed organizing with some fun times, so it was not all work. We shared the experience with other family members who could pop in and help here and there. Some tasks were outsourced to others, and some items were hauled off for donation. If there is no family or friend to help, remember, we go solo as part of Earth Adventures For Kids mindset and we forge our own path. You can reach out to businesses, organizations, charities, churches, clubs, and other community support to help you.

✓ **Find treasures** to place into your TLC Save Forever Box(es), TLC Journal/Binder(s), and Catch-All Bag(s). When you start clearing out "stuff and piles" you will find treasures you want to save, so have your containers ready for them.

✓ **Professional organizing is a skill that can be learned and practiced.** Some fight it and resist, but you can learn to see what's possible if you change the space around and de-clutter. Plan how to approach clearing the space. Place only what is useful, enjoyable, and needed back in the space. Then, you can ensure that your surroundings and physical spaces are helping you and not hindering you.

✓ **Create a "vision board" of what you like.** Look at different magazines, catalogs, and websites to develop ideas. Determine what style you like, your budget, and your level of need. I have mixed in a few expensive decorative storage cabinets with mostly less expensive storage solutions in my house.

✓ **We have found that the key to organizing is having containers**—especially containers you like and enjoy, and that have great features like stack-ability. Containers come in many forms and can be decorative wooden cabinets, a wooden chest, free-standing shelving units, cupboards, closets, bins, plastic baggies, and so on. I prefer closed decorative cabinets, so I do not have to dust a lot of knick-knacks. I also have many "cubby style" cube shelving units that look good with a mixture of bins, baskets, books, art, and knick-knacks in the cubbies. Containers can be shelving units with decorative bins or baskets on the shelves. The cube shelving units offer the ability to have a combination of decorative bins and baskets. Put books in one cube and other treasures in another so the unit has a collection mix of bins, books, art, and knick-knacks. Go to the websites of companies like IKEA, Pottery Barn, Grandin Road, California Closets, Restoration Hardware, The Container Store, Home Depot, Overstock, and World Market Cost Plus to get inspiration for your vision.

✓ **Budgets:** Sometimes our budgets feel like they limit what we want to do. I have found that having a clear vision of what I like helps me find it and get it at a price I can afford. Stores have sales, so you can watch for sales. If you tend to over-buy, and hoard, maybe shopping for new items is not what you need to be doing if you are trying to de-clutter. Recruit someone to help you selectively shop and decide what works for your space without overbuying or buying things that do not work in the space.

✓ **Decide your plan of approach.** Choose one space at a time. Begin sorting and deciding on one part of the space, and make your way through each drawer, cabinet, closet, and cubby. Some sections will be easier than others. Clear plastic containers help with easy sorting while going through the process. Have multiple Catch-All Bags on hand, too. And, of course, have plenty of clean trash bags and cardboard boxes available during the sorting process. Decide if a "clean-slate-batch-dump-into-a-storage-container" is best for the space.

✓ **If you are in a phase of life in which your loved ones may need to step in and help** with your assets and liabilities at one point soon in the future, have discussions with them on what they would like to see in your spaces as the tasks will fall on them when they need to step in to assist. Value their input and find out what you can do now to help them make this time of stepping in easier on them. You can make the plan and define the steps together.

✓ **You can print all the bullet point lists, checklists, and worksheets in this book, put them on a clipboard,** and use them as a guide during the phases of TLC creation. These itemized lists can help as quick references and reminders to you and others. If you reach an impasse or a place where it seems you are stuck, refer to these bullet point lists to help you get unstuck.

✓ **It may seem that some of the information in this book repeats, and it does—but for good reason!** We are training the brain with new information through repetition and every list in this book is slightly different in format and information.

✓ **How does the TLC Method** of Mindset, Tools, Systems, and Marketplace apply to the particular space and/or situation you are working in? As you work through your "stuff and piles" ask yourself if a new mindset, or new tools, systems, and marketplace products and services can help in the space.

A word on the gifting of your treasures . . .

As part of your TLC cleaning, you can give items to others that you would like them to have in your memory as an heirloom. When you've chosen someone to give an item to, discuss the item(s) with them and see if they have room for it, need it, or want it. **This process can be emotional,** especially if the prized possession you treasure may not be to your loved one's taste, or they may not have room to store it. Do your best not to be offended. Each person goes through life collecting their own "treasures" and may be unable to store or use the item on offer.

Try to diffuse the emotion and attachment to objects if others do not share the same appreciation. This is just a part of life that we all have to come to terms with. I don't expect my kids to want a "gold eagle medallion" that represents something special to my mom's extended family and friends. Nor do I expect them to embrace all the knick-knacks collected by my grandma from thrift stores. Where would they store it all? I have kept some of my grandma's dish collections, but I can only keep what works for my household.

Years ago, my sister and I inherited a lot of stuff from some family friends. We could not possibly store it, nor did we treasure it. Navigating emotions around stuff is a complicated issue with which we all must come to terms if we are going through our items and want to gift some items to others. The process of gifting treasures needs to be discussed.

MAKE AN EVENT OF THE LETTING GO OF TREASURES.

You can honor the items and what they represent to you by having a special event or occasion that marks "the letting go of items" as a milestone—passing them on in a special way. You can have a photographer take pictures and videos of you all with the items so you can have quality photos to mark this special occasion and the treasure(s) along with the history documented and the stories of why the item(s) is special to you. Those photos and videos can go in your Treasure Legacy Collection with the stories preserving the significance and passing them on to future generations. This brings me to my next point.

TAKE A PICTURE; IT LASTS LONGER!

I learned that the difficult decisions of what to do with my kids' stuff when they outgrew it was handled better when **I realized I could take multiple pictures of the items and always remember them with pictures.** This made it easier to donate or sell and part with the object that had become an integration of my life story. I decided which of their toys and childhood memorabilia I would like to keep based on the value of it, the quality, and the likelihood we would use it again when they have kids. I considered my ability to store the items without causing "stuff and piles" clutter in my own household.

I am so happy to be able to appreciate, in photograph form, the treasured items I gave away or sold. It gives me joy looking at the photos of the treasured items and I can share the photos with others. You could create a Canva collage with certain pictures of treasures you decided to pass on to others.

Having a digital picture to remember the items gives you a sense of always having the item, making it easier to part with so you can get on with creating your new spaces!

On the other hand, don't be hasty and give away too much that you may regret later. For example, we gave away a collection of my grandma's costume jewelry and buttons for sewing, not knowing that, later, our teenage daughter would get crafty and would love to use her grandma's collection of buttons and costume jewelry.

EXPAND YOUR THINKING AND PERSPECTIVES.

In addition to all the TLC cleaning, estate planning, and life planning techniques, tips, and ideas we have discussed in this book, **we believe it is worthwhile and advantageous to look to other cultures, religions, and people in different time periods** for their different ways of dealing with life and passing into the next life, bridging the gap between Heaven and Earth.

Perhaps in researching your own ancestry and ancestral customs, you may find some additional meaningful traditions to add to your Treasure Legacy Collection. For example, we have Hawaiian heritage and DNA. Although we are not aware of the customs and traditions of the Hawaiians because we are removed from the knowledge, we may find some information and practices that resonate with us that we want to include in our TLC.

Here are two wonderful examples of learning from other cultures:

1. **Look up "Ghana funerals" online** and read about the funeral traditions of Ghana. Author Sarah Kessler discusses the different practices in her article *Ghanaian Funerals: Traditions & What to Expect* posted here https://www.joincake.com/blog/ghana-funeral/.

2. **Look up the term "Swedish death cleaning" online.** Read books and articles to get the gist of Swedish death cleaning; it is similar to our TLC cleaning, both dealing with "getting affairs in order" and enjoying treasures and items with your loved ones now and today.

I choose to make this process of TLC cleaning enjoyable and a part of life rather than a somber and sad experience. I do not wait to do my TLC cleanings because different phases of life require that we keep clearing out the old phase to make way for the new phase. I look back on the old phase and acknowledge the benefits, milestones, and blessings, and then I look forward to the new phase and the incoming benefits, milestones, and blessings. Having some sort of special moment or event marking the change in phase from old to new is beneficial. After our kids were grown, we were on vacation and the resort pool had a waterfall. I told my husband, let's swim through the waterfall at the same time and let the past phase of life go, and we entered our new phase of life! I have looked back at that moment a few times and it has helped me keep moving forward!

ARTICLES ON SWEDISH DEATH CLEANING CAN HELP YOU WITH YOUR OWN TLC PROCESS:

https://www.thespruce.com/swedish-death-cleaning-4801461

https://www.familyhandyman.com/list/10-things-to-know-about-swedish-death-cleaning/

https://www.realsimple.com/home-organizing/organizing/what-is-swedish-death-cleaning

https://www.bhg.com/decorating/storage/organization-basics/swedish-death-cleaning-tips/

https://www.dumpsters.com/blog/how-to-do-swedish-death-cleaning

From *The Gentle Art of Swedish Death Cleaning* book description:

https://www.amazon.com/Gentle-Art-Swedish-Death-Cleaning/dp/1501173243

"A charming, practical, and unsentimental approach to putting a home in order while reflecting on the tiny joys that make up a long life.

In Sweden, there is a kind of decluttering called döstädning, dö meaning 'death' and städning meaning 'cleaning.' This surprising and invigorating process of clearing out unnecessary belongings can be undertaken at any age or life stage but should be done sooner than later before others have to do it for you. In The Gentle Art of Swedish Death Cleaning, artist Margareta Magnusson, with Scandinavian humor and wisdom, instructs readers to embrace minimalism. Her radical and joyous method for putting things in order helps families broach sensitive conversations and makes the process uplifting rather than overwhelming.

Margareta suggests which possessions you can easily get rid of (unworn clothes, unwanted presents, more plates than you'd ever use) and which you might want to keep (photographs, love letters, a few of your children's art projects). Digging into her late husband's tool shed and her own secret drawer of vices, Margareta introduces an element of fun to a potentially daunting task. Along the way, readers get a glimpse into her life in Sweden and **become more comfortable with the idea of letting go**.

Margareta Magnusson is, in her own words, aged between 80 and 100. Born in Sweden, she has lived all over the world. Margareta graduated from Beckman's College of Design, and her art has been exhibited in galleries from Hong Kong to Singapore. She has five children and lives in Stockholm. She is the author of The Gentle Art of Swedish Death Cleaning and The Swedish Art of Aging Well."

Another helpful book to check out:

- *Your Space Made Simple* by Ariel Magidson https://www.penguinrandomhouse.com/books/720719/your-space-made-simple-by-ariel-magidson/

CHAPTER 10

SOME CONCLUDING THOUGHTS, DEFINITIONS, AND MORE

We have discussed estate planning, life planning, and TLC as a way of life. We have explored creating a Treasure Legacy Collection and why it benefits you and others. This chapter will wrap up with random, relevant points and helpful definitions for you to ponder.

REGARDING MORE FORMAL ESTATE PLANNING:

Botti and Morison Estate Planning Attorneys, https://bottilaw.com/, is one of the best firms we have found. If you can attend one of their virtual or in-person workshops on estate planning for the learning factor, do so. If you are outside California, they may have a recommended referral to a similar firm.

We are not endorsing them; rather, we're sharing their website as a useful tool to see what they include in their estate planning, and you might decide to consult with them. Their ultimate goal is to protect you and your loved ones from probate and have an effective "passing of assets" to beneficiaries. They streamline the process and set it up, so you do not always have to update your Living Trust every time you buy or sell an asset.

On our accounts, when possible, we declare beneficiaries, and we annually check our account beneficiary status. A key point to this is having these accounts and assets organized in your TLC Journal/Binder, as well as having your Financial Worksheet completed, which you can read about in our book, *How to Create a Financial Worksheet.*

We may also consider co-ownership with an adult child as a limited owner having restrictions on taking any actions, but ownership would go to that person in the event of our departing this Earth.

We also like Certified Public Accountant (CPA) and Tax Attorney, Mark J. Kohler, for his helpful information on taxes, assets, estate planning, and more. Here is some of his work, and you can join his free email list as he has a podcast, free webinars, and informative articles.

From Mark J. Kohler's email newsletter article ***Four Reasons You NEED a Trust*** and related video that you can find on YouTube:

"**1. Wealth Building**: The foundation of your wealth building needs to be a trust. We recommend starting with a *Revocable Living Trust.*

2. Privacy: Properly naming a trust and allocating your assets to it is the first step toward privacy.

3. Avoiding Probate: A trust is where all your assets gather and can be divided easily without involving judges and courts. A will cannot do that.

4. Rules of Distribution: With a trust, you can set up rules of distribution, where you can set how the money should be spent and when!"

He continues in the email newsletter, "See the benefits of having a KKOS Lawyer draft a specialized estate plan to help your family. You'll find information about a comprehensive estate plan here, https://kkoslawyers.com/services/comprehensive-estate-plan/.

We wish no one would ever have to experience the passing of a loved one. However, it happens, and because of that, we want to ensure everyone has their past, present, and future secured."

From an email newsletter I received by Mark J. Kohler declaring **"Leave a plan, not chaos, for your loved ones"** he states:

"Unlike a will, a trust can distribute your legacy on YOUR terms. Is your child too young or immature to receive their entire inheritance? From yearly payments to drug tests, you set the level of controls on their inheritance when it's established in a trust. You can even set conditions on how the money is spent, such as on their first home or college! Explore more ways to take control of your trust from the video **Take Control of Your Legacy, Get Your Trust in Order.**"

We consulted with and followed the advice of at least three different attorneys and accountants. We reviewed their suggestions and cross-referenced information. Then we decided who we wanted to work with and how we wanted to proceed. You can research and find your own legal, tax, and financial advisors. When I was 20, I took a financial planning course, and I was surprised to find out that an important part of financial planning is buying insurance policies—so add insurance agents to your team of advisors. Ask others for referrals to help you find quality advisors.

TREASURE LEGACY COLLECTION VOCABULARY TO PONDER.

These first three definitions are from The American Heritage® Dictionary of the English Language, 5th Edition:

Definition of ESSENCE: The intrinsic or indispensable quality or qualities that serve to characterize or identify something. The inherent, unchanging nature of a thing or class of things. The most important part or aspect of something. *Think of putting your essence into your TLC.*

Definition of BEING: The state or quality of having existence: synonym: existence. The totality of all things that exist. A person. *Think of putting the overall sense of your being into your TLC.*

Definition of ZEST: Flavor. Interest or excitement. *Think of putting your zest for life into your TLC.*

Definition of MOJO: A power that may seem magical and allows someone to be very effective and successful. https://www.britannica.com/ *Think of putting your mojo into your TLC.*

Definition of TREASURE: Per vocabulary.com: "Treasure is usually associated with riches—gold, jewels, doubloons—the stuff contained in pirates' treasure chests. However, you can also treasure things with purely sentimental value—like your pet rock from childhood or your blankie. Our son loved the sticks he collected as a child, and we saved them for a time, but as he grew up, we let the sticks go back to nature! The English word treasure comes from the Old French tresor, both meaning "something of great worth." Still, the French tresor sounds so much more luxurious than the English treasure, and that form is the chosen name for an expensive perfume. Worth is relative, though. Going back further, we find that the Latin word for treasury is thesaurus, which is what a book of synonyms is called. Guess the ancients always understood the richness and worth of words."

The goal of the Treasure Legacy Collection is to help you easily collect your treasures, safely keep them, and create easy-to-access methods and formats, helping you live your legacy every day. It allows others to enjoy your treasured legacy as well. The Treasure Legacy Collection helps you breathe more life into your day-to-day life and estate plan.

Our goal is to help you create a legacy that captures your mojo, essence, energy, and zest for life, and to communicate it in a way that is easy for others to enjoy. Bring others into your lifestyle by creating your Treasure Legacy Collection to improve relationships, grow influence, improve communications, and live your best life today while creating cords of comfort that bridge the gap between Heaven and Earth.

The following statements are from the Legacy Law Advisors website www.legacylawadvisors.com:

"A legacy is defined as something that is passed on. But legacy can take many forms.

- A legacy may be of one's faith, ethics, and core values.

- A legacy may be monetary or your assets.

- A legacy may come from one's character, reputation, and the life you lead—setting an example for others and guiding their futures.

- Legacies often tremendously impact, encourage, and leave pathways for future generations.

- Legacies guide and inspire family members and those affected by you to live lives that impact their faith, homes, community, and businesses."

THINK OF CREATING YOUR LEGACY AS A WAY OF LIVING YOUR LIFE TO THE FULLEST.

TLC Method Reminders:

- **Tell your stories in a simple format.** Share what you overcame in life and how, and how you helped others overcome. Include who, what, when, where, how, and why. Stories can simply be fun moments in life you want to share. Your 5 TLC Legacy Lists become the basis for your stories, so write your 5 TLC Legacy Lists before you write your stories.

- **Write your Activities in My Name List.** Use our book *101 Things to Do Other Than Social Media* as prompts and ideas for what to do, with whom, and when making memories now with your loved ones. Use the book and the list you generate to guide those who carry on in your name, your spirit, and your mojo in the future. Place your list in your TLC Save Forever Box or TLC Journal/Binder. Use this list to do activities today, improving your life and legacy.

- **Write your Values and Pillars List.** Use our book *A Series of Unsuspecting Children's Poems* for prompts on wisdom pieces, advice, guidance, thoughts, and experiences to type up and place your list into your TLC Journal/Binder or TLC Save Forever Box. Use this list to have meaningful conversations today.

- **Write your Cozy and Comforting Nights List.** Use our book *When the Sun Goes Down: How to Enjoy the Night* for prompts on how to enjoy the hours between twilight and dawn. Store the list in your TLC Journal/Binder or TLC Save Forever Box. You can also use a copy to keep handy as a reminder of activities to do with your loved ones now to improve your relationships. Use this list to make your nights better and to create cords of comfort, improving relationships now.

- **Write your Financial Nuts and Bolts List.** Use our book *How to Create a Financial Worksheet* for prompts on financial organization and store your list in your TLC Journal/Binder or TLC Save Forever Box so others will have important information in case they need to step in to assist you with finances. Use this list to ensure you have your "ducks in a row" instead of "chickens scattered here and there." Take action on important items in your finances to reap rewards.

- **Write your Health and Wellness List.** Use our book *Earth Adventures For Kids Fitness* for prompts on health and wellness to communicate to others what you value in terms of health and wellness. Store your list in your TLC Save Forever Box or TLC Journal/Binder. You can print this list and give it to loved ones, using the list to do activities now.

- **The Marketplace on our website at** www.EarthAdventuresForKids.com will help you with additional prompts for your 5 TLC Legacy Lists above as The Marketplace is full of products and services that help with activities, values and pillars, nighttime, finances, and health and wellness. Use the power of engaging with The Marketplace to write your 5 TLC Legacy Lists and to improve your life and legacy.

- **Use Canva Pro** to create fun presentations, collages, videos, cards, and more with photos, graphics, captions, and headlines. Digitize old, print photos, and share the creations and digitized photos with others.

- **Use the TLC Save Forever Box** for keeping items/info like the following: your recipe box, favorites of whatever you enjoy, favorite TV shows, songs, music, artists, activities, holiday celebration information, traditions, favorite movies, places to go and see, favorite comedians, and keepsakes. **A quick note on the classic "recipe box" and recipes handed down through the generations:** A loved one who immigrated to America from Mexico in the early 1900s had a recipe for salsa. Our son takes great pleasure in making this salsa recipe, and it brings to life memories and appreciation of Louie, who brought the recipe to his new homeland. Our son has enjoyed making this salsa with other family members as a way of continuing on in Louie's essence, spirit, zest, and mojo. It's hot salsa!

- **Use The Wondering Mat** as a place of comfort and healing to remember loved ones and gain inspiration, strength, and peace. Use the mat as a place of transformation, imagination, overcoming, and rising above. You can always buy an extra Wondering Mat and keep it rolled up in your TLC Save Forever Box for loved ones to enjoy in the future in your absence.

- **Use The Megaphone** on outings for effective communication and use it to make your "sort and decide through the stuff and piles" organization process fun. You can use it in many other ways as discussed in our book *How to Create Your Own Signature Collection.* We like the smaller-sized megaphones with a hand strap and volume control.

- **Use different sizes of Catch-All Bags and the nesting bags concept** to help with separating categories, doing activities, grouping like-items, and to help you be ready for a variety of situations.

- **Create your own traditions** like making punch or writing an annual one-page newsletter, maybe in wintertime or on a special holiday. Highlight key points of last year, add some fun graphics, and fonts with color, laminate it, and you will over the years you will have a history book!

- **Focus on** health, wealth, relationships with loved ones, experiences, and whatever ways you can share more quality time together, even if you are far apart.

- **Go solo** on your TLC when you want to or need to. The solo processes of your TLC are very rewarding, and you will meet others along the way. Join our email list to get notified of events, updates, and resources for the solo TLC.

- **Buy digital copies of our books and the print version from Amazon.** With the digital copies, you can print the quizzes, checklists, bullet point lists, and worksheets to use in the TLC creation process. With the printed books, you can give them as gifts to others and keep copies to include in your TLC for future generations.

- **View the pictures on our website to see various components of the TLC in use**.

- Track your TLC progress with the checklists included in this book.

- Download our free quizzes at ForParents.EarthAdventuresForKids.com or print them from the digital copy of this book. Complete the quizzes to help determine if you need our coaching.

- **Join our email list** to be notified of new releases, how-to videos, and special offers. We will also host webinars for low-cost group coaching, so be sure to join our email list to get notified of these opportunities.

Because I expect your life today to improve when you create your Treasure Legacy Collection, I am motivated and inspired to hear how it benefits you and improves your life. You can submit your positive and uplifting success stories to us at our email address:

Hello@EarthAdventuresForKids.com.

CHAPTER 11

NEXT STEPS - IS COACHING FOR YOU? TAKE OUR QUIZ AND USE OUR CHECKLISTS AND WORKSHEETS

The checklists, bullet point lists, worksheets, and quizzes in this book can help you progress through creating a TLC. The information is often repeated in different formats, and you can print the pages from your digital copy of this book, put them on a clipboard, and use them to help you keep on track and make progress. On our websites, go to the coaching section to learn more about how we can help you stay focused, move through the process in a manageable way, get your TLC Legacy Lists written, your stories written, and get your TLC done and incorporated into your daily lifestyle with ease. Your legacy lifestyle with our TLC Method can start today!

We have ways to help you write your 5 TLC Legacy Lists and Tell Your Stories. Go to ForParents. EarthAdventuresForKids.com and www.EarthAdventuresForKids.com to learn more about:

★ Our low-cost monthly subscription service to help you create your TLC.

★ One-on-one 90-day Coaching Programs.

★ We will also host webinars for low-cost group coaching, so be sure to join our email list to get notified of these opportunities.

WELCOME TO OUR QUIZ SECTION

The self-reflection quizzes below are for informational purposes only. They are designed to help you identify if you are effectively organized so you experience the joy of being on "**an upward spiral**" in life. When we are on an upward spiral in life, we tend to have better days and nights as most areas are "humming along" in a way that works for us.

Do you have an area of life that could be improved? Great! Most of us have these areas.

If you have an area you feel might be in "a downward spiral," you can take organization and habit steps to hypothetically "find an oar and place it in the water" to get going in the direction you want to go. You are always the "captain of your own ship;" we are simply showing you tools that have helped us become wildly successful—not perfect, but successful according to our own definition of success. You can decide what tools to implement in your household and what works for you, creating your own unique systems.

At Earth Adventures For Kids, we focus on the TLC Method of Mindset, Tools, Systems, and Marketplace. Our books, products, and services offer organizational and positive discipline ideas that you can choose from to create your own unique Signature Collection that facilitates your mode of operation and how you do you!

We also offer the same books, products, and services from an additional perspective, and different lens for creating your Treasure Legacy Collection, as explained in our books. Read our two foundational books *How to Create Your Own Signature Collection: The Ultimate Guide to Improving Your Life and Legacy* and *How to Create a Treasure Legacy Collection: The Ultimate Guide to Living Your Best Life Now.*

We have three quizzes below, each based on our books. We offer coaching options if you want additional support and assistance in accomplishing your goals. You can write your answers on a separate sheet of paper for your eyes only. Please make sure to read our copyright page and disclaimers. By continuing to read our books, you acknowledge and accept our releases of liability.

QUIZ #1: SIGNATURE COLLECTION QUIZ:

This quiz is based on our book, *How to Create Your Own Signature Collection: The Ultimate Guide to Improving Your Life and Legacy* which is available in digital download and print.

1. Overall, do your days and nights flow how you want them to flow?

2. Overall, are your home and office places where you feel they are "in order," allowing you to accomplish what you want to accomplish?

3. Overall, do you feel that your organization and systems in your finances, such as bill pay, income stream(s), and debt load, are manageable so that you often celebrate wins?

4. Overall, do you feel your relationships have "good times" on the menu? In the array of your life's activities and events, are good times often a part of it all?

5. Overall, do you feel that your health and wellness are fine-tuned with enough sleep, sustained energy through the day, quality mental focus and that you generally feel good?

6. Overall, do you feel you have a great level of "quality of life" experiences?

7. Is there an event(s) that caused you to "lose your mode of operation and balance," and you need to do something different now to get where you want to be?

8. Do you want to improve any of the above areas?

9. Do you think our coaching programs will help you reach your goals faster?

10. How can the TLC Method be applied? For this specific space or situation, what is the mindset? What are the tools used? What are the systems in place? What are the products and services from the marketplace that can improve the space?

11. Visit our page **ForParents.EarthAdventuresForKids.com** and scroll down to read about our coaching programs. *Coaching is for organization purposes only. We do not give professional advice, and we recommend you consult with your professional advisors, including health and wellness advisors, as needed.*

QUIZ #2: TREASURE LEGACY COLLECTION QUIZ:

This quiz is based on our book, *How to Create a Treasure Legacy Collection: The Ultimate Guide to Living Your Best Life Now,* which is available in digital and print.

1. Overall, do you feel that your "ducks are in a row," meaning that you have important information ready for others in the event of an emergency?

2. Is your important information in easy-to-identify, labeled containers such as bins, bags, binders, journals, files, et cetera, so that anyone can see that they are important and part of your legacy and estate plan?

3. Does your current estate plan go beyond the standard basics and include parts of you that you want your loved ones to know and help bridge the gap between heaven and earth while strengthening bonds between you and your loved ones now?

4. Overall, do you feel that you and your loved ones enjoy "quality of life" moments in which you have time together doing meaningful activities?

5. When you reflect on your life, do you want more or less of those past experiences and reference points?

6. When you look forward to your future, do you have a "vision board" of what you want to experience and accomplish and with whom? Do you see ways in which living your best life today helps you build the legacy you want?

7. How do you go about living your best life today?

8. Have you experienced the loss of a loved one for whom you would like to create a Treasure Legacy Collection in their memory?

9. Is there a loved one, perhaps an elderly parent, for whom you would like to create a Treasure Legacy Collection now as a way of improving life and legacy while they are still with us on earth and bridging the gap between heaven and earth for when the time comes for their earth departure?

10. Would you like to create a Treasure Legacy Collection for yourself with your loved ones as a way of improving relationships and quality of life?

11. How can the TLC Method be applied? For this specific space or situation, what is the mindset? What are the tools used? What are the systems in place? What are the products and services from the marketplace that can improve the space?

12. Do you think our coaching programs will help you reach your goals faster?

13. Visit our page **ForParents.EarthAdventuresForKids.com** and scroll down to read about our coaching programs. *Coaching is for organization purposes only and is not financial, legal, or estate planning advice. We recommend consulting with your legal, estate planning, tax, and financial advisors when needed.*

QUIZ #3: THE FINANCIAL WORKSHEET QUIZ:

This quiz is based on our book *How to Create a Financial Worksheet,* which is available in digital and print. This is not tax or financial advice; the book is for organizing purposes only.

1. Overall, do you feel like you are often "a day late and a dollar short?"

2. Overall, do you feel that you have a sense that you are "winning" the day in terms of being on time or early in payments, benefiting from opportunities, eliminating financial habits that are not helping you reach your goals, and so forth?

3. Overall, are your taxes and inflation manageable, or do you feel there could be an improvement?

4. Do you have a "dream team" of tax and financial professionals that assist you in reaching your goals?

5. Is debt an issue in your financial picture?

6. Overall, do you know what the state of your financial picture is every day?

7. Overall, do you feel excited about looking at your finances, or do you get a feeling of dread?

8. Is there an event(s) that caused you to "lose your mode of operation and balance," and you need to do something different now to get where you want to be?

9. How can the TLC Method be applied? For this specific space or situation, what is the mindset? What are the tools used? What are the systems in place? What are the products and services from the marketplace that can improve the space?

10. Do you think our coaching programs will help you reach your goals faster?

11. Visit our page **ForParents.EarthAdventuresForKids.com** and scroll down to read about our coaching programs. *Coaching is for financial organization purposes only. This is not financial advice; we recommend you consult with your tax and financial advisors.*

Share the link to **ForParents.EarthAdventuresForKids.com** so others can download our Free Quiz and opt-in to our community to receive updates about events, special offers, and new releases.

Earth Adventures For Kids Informational Quizzes

CHECKLIST OF OUR PRODUCTS
FOR YOUR TLC TRANSFORMATION THROUGH ORGANIZATION

☐ **READ OUR BOOKS AND MAKE YOUR 5 TLC LEGACY LISTS.**
Create and implement your own action items based on the information in our books.

- **Foundational Book 1:** *How to Create Your Own Signature Collection: The Ultimate Guide to Improving Your Life and Legacy*

- **Foundational Book 2:** *How to Create a Treasure Legacy Collection: The Ultimate Guide to Living Your Best Life Now*

- **Book:** *101 Things to Do Other than Social Media*; use it to write your Activities in My Name List

- **Book:** *A Series of Unsuspecting Children's Poems*; use it to write your Values and Pillars List

- **Book:** *How to Create a Financial Worksheet*; use it to write your Financial Nuts and Bolts List

- **Book:** *When the Sun Goes Down: How to Enjoy the Night*; use it to write your Cozy and Comforting Nights List

- **Book:** *Earth Adventures For Kids Fitness*; use it to write your Health and Wellness List

- **Join our Marketplace Annual Membership:** Use it to write your Health and Wellness List, Values and Pillars List, Financial Nuts and Bolts List, Cozy and Comforting Nights List, and Activities in My Name List.

☐ **BUY OUR LABELS AND SOURCE YOUR CONTAINERS.**
Containers with proper labels are key to getting organized. Buy our labels and source your containers.

- **Label:** Save Forever Box—this is explained in our Signature Collection book.

- **Container:** Save Forever Box—this is explained in our Signature Collection book.

- **Label:** TLC Save Forever Box

- **Container:** TLC Save Forever Box

- **Label:** TLC Journal/Binder

- **Container:** TLC Journal/Binder

- **Container:** The Catch-All Bag

☐ **BUY OUR WONDERING MAT AND USE TO RENEW, RESET, CALM.**
A Tool for Transformation: The Wondering Mat—With the TLC, your mat can be used during times of remembering your loved one(s) allowing profound inner experiences to take place.

☐ **GET YOUR MEGAPHONE FOR EFFECTIVE, FUN COMMUNICATION.**

A Tool for Communication: The Megaphone—With the TLC, your megaphone can be used on outings and during the "Sorting and Deciding of the Stuff and Piles" process. Make it fun! Read our book *How to Create Your Own Signature Collection: The Ultimate Guide to Improving Your Life and Legacy* for more information on how fun and powerful The Megaphone can be. We like the smaller-sized megaphones with a hand strap and volume control. You can also read about it and view helpful images of megaphone use at www.EarthAdventuresForKids.com under Shop. **We recommend megaphone use only for adults; kids can respect it as a tool used by caregivers.**

☐ **REACH YOUR GOALS FASTER WITH OUR HELP.**

Check out our webinar group coaching, low-cost monthly subscription coaching, and one-on-one 90-day Coaching Programs. We help you use our tools to reach your goals and improve your life and legacy! We will host webinars for low-cost group coaching, so be sure to join our email list to get notified of these opportunities. Go to our website page at ForParents.EarthAdventuresForKids.com to learn more about our coaching options.

TREASURE LEGACY COLLECTION TLC METHOD CHECKLIST

☐ **Read this book, *How to Create a Treasure Legacy Collection,* in its entirety and take notes.** Commit to getting to know the tools in the Treasure Legacy Collection and know why you want to create a TLC. Print all the quizzes, checklists, bullet lists, and worksheets and then put them on a clipboard to refer to during the TLC creation process.

☐ **Buy all the items in the Treasure Legacy Collection.** Make sure to buy the labels for both the TLC Save Forever Box and the TLC Journal/Binder. They are sold in single quantities at our site ForParents.EarthAdventuresForKids.com, and we recommend buying two to four or more at a time, depending on how many containers you have.

☐ **Inform loved ones you will be creating a Treasure Legacy Collection.** Invite them to join you for all or part of the process. If they cannot, that is okay! You can ask again in the future. You can also ask friends or pay for some of the tasks to be completed. Go solo if you need to or want to! Join our email list to be notified of new releases and events.

☐ **Put the TLC labels on your TLC Save Forever Box and your TLC Journal/Binder.** Have "places for the spaces" meaning have all types of containers ready to sort items into. Catch-All Bags with the nesting options in the TLC-creating process. These are the "places for your spaces."

☐ **Live your legacy every day.** Begin implementing the tools and system into your days and nights by picking and choosing what works for you and using your own ideas as well. Have your TLC Save Forever Box containers, TLC Journal/Binder, and Catch-All Bags ready to go, and when you come across items you want to be part of your TLC, just place them in the correct container.

☐ Type up your **Activities in My Name List.** Share it with loved ones and direct them to do these things/activities with you in mind. They can pick and choose the activities that work for them. You can do the activities together now, and when you depart, they can continue in your name and spirit. Use the book *101 Things to Do Other Than Social Media* as inspiration and a guide. You can store a copy of this list in your TLC Save Forever Box and/or your TLC Journal/Binder. You can send a copy to loved ones so they have a copy handy, and they can add it to their TLC.

☐ **Type up your Values and Pillars List for loved ones.** You can share the list for meaningful conversations now to help you have those conversations with loved ones. Store a copy of your list in your TLC Save Forever Box and/or Journal/Binder. Use the book *A Series of Unsuspecting Children's Poems* as inspiration and a guide. You can send a copy of your list to loved ones so they have a copy handy, and they can add it to their TLC.

☐ **Type up your Cozy and Comforting Nights List.** Share it with loved ones for meaningful conversations now. You can do some of the activities together now, and in the future, they can carry on in your name and spirit. Use the book *When the Sun Goes Down: How to Enjoy the Night* as your inspiration and guide. You can send a copy of your list to loved ones so they have a copy handy, and they can add it to their TLC.

☐ **Type up your Financial Nuts and Bolts List.** Share it with loved ones. You can include what you have learned and what has benefited you in the world of finance. This could even be a list of what NOT to do learned from your "school of hard knocks!" Use the book *How to Create a Financial Worksheet* as your guide. Keep a copy of your list in your TLC Save Forever Box and/or TLC Journal/Binder. You can send a copy of your list to loved ones so they have a copy handy, and they can add it to their TLC.

☐ **Type up your Health and Wellness List.** Share it with loved ones. You can include what you have learned and what has benefited you in the realm of health and wellness. Use the book, *Earth Adventures For Kids Fitness.* Keep a copy of your list in your TLC Save Forever Box and/ or TLC Journal/Binder. You can send a copy to loved ones so they have a copy handy, and they can add it to their TLC.

☐ **Use The Marketplace to add to your 5 TLC Legacy Lists.** The Marketplace can be a source of additional information to include on your lists. Make your TLC Legacy Lists personal and add your own style. You might want to include special family information and what has worked for you in life, allowing you to live your best life.

☐ **Place items in your labeled TLC Save Forever Box, TLC Journal/Binder when you are ready.** Use Catch-All Bags as needed through the TLC-creating process. It is helpful when you are in the sorting the "**sorting and deciding of the stuff and piles**" phase to have lots of extra Catch-All Bags and containers as you decide what to keep, toss/recycle, give away, and sell. Remember, you can use the nesting "bags in bags" concept to make rummaging through your stored items easier in the future.

☐ **Learn new technology.** Let technology assist you in creating an enjoyable, organized, easy-to-use TLC. Use Canva Pro and digitize old photos.

☐ **Go through each room in your house**. Do TLC cleaning throughout each cupboard, drawer, closet, garage, shed, storage container, cabinet, et cetera. Pace yourself. Maybe do one room each month. **Have your containers on hand, ready to go:** TLC Save Forever Boxes, empty storage containers, plastic trash bags, Catch-All Bags, cardboard boxes, and Ziploc baggies of all sizes. You might even need to rent a trailer or U-Haul in which to place the donate-give away-and-toss items. Sort through and place items in an appropriate container. **Decide: Keep, Give Away, Sell, Toss/Recycle.** Hire help if needed. Ask for help if needed. Make it as enjoyable as possible. Remember your key benefits, vision board mindset, and guiding principles mindset to help move you through the "slogging through/drudgery" parts. You can document the process with before, during, and after photos. Take pictures of "difficult to part with items" and make an event of parting with them—enjoy the photos in the future.

☐ **Practice using the TLC Method as a way of life.** Follow these steps:

1. Print all the checklists and worksheets in this book. Keep them on a clipboard to refer to when getting familiar with the TLC Method and Legacy Lifestyle. After a time, with practice, you will be so familiar with all the components of your TLC, that you will naturally incorporate them into daily life; this is the point when you will be living your best life with TLC!

2. Create memories by doing activities and having meaningful conversations now by taking the action steps outlined in the TLC.

3. Type up your 5 TLC Legacy Lists using our books. Give these lists to loved ones. Use the lists on a regular basis as action items to create cords of comfort, create memories, and improve life and relationships.

4. Organize your home, office, and finances. Manage incoming, outgoing, and storage for items in each space.

5. Continue to add to your TLC Save Forever Box and TLC Journal/Binder as desired.

6. Continue to invite loved ones to join you in the activities and components of living the TLC lifestyle.

7. Go solo with your TLC when you want to or need to.

☐ **Practice reframing situations into the most positive light.** Practice receiving inspiration first and then giving inspiration to life situations and people every day. Become a pillar in your life for others in your household, family, and community. Another source to check out on this topic is the book *Just Look Up: Five Life-Saving Phrases Every Human Needs to Hear* by Joe Beckman, https://justlookupbook.com/. The book helps us remember the simple power of acknowledging each other with our words, smiles, and eye contact. It reminds me of the word "namaste," which basically means that I acknowledge the divine in me and the divine in you, by which we are connected.

CHECKLIST FOR MY COMPLETED TLC

Print multiple copies of this checklist and mark the boxes when complete. Then insert this completed checklist into the front cover of your TLC Journal/Binder or as the first page. Keep a copy in your TLC Save Forever Box too. Sign up for the low-cost monthly subscription or one-on-one 90-day Coaching Programs if you would like our assistance moving through the TLC process.

☐ Read the book *How to Create a Treasure Legacy Collection*.

☐ Inform friends and family that I am creating a TLC and invite them to join me.

☐ Buy all the tools in the TLC, including the TLC labels.

☐ Get familiar with all the tools by reading all the TLC books and Journal Stories on the Journal page of www.EarthAdventuresForKids.com.

☐ Buy all my containers including the TLC Save Forever Box, the TLC Journal/Binder, and the TLC labels for each.

☐ Get tech savvy with Canva and old photo digitization with a smartphone and email.

☐ Room by room, closet by closet, drawer by drawer, do a TLC cleaning in my house and garage.

☐ Using the book, *101 Things to Do Other Than Social Media*, write my **Activities in My Name List** and store it in my labeled TLC Save Forever Box(es) and/or TLC Journal /Binder(s). Use this list for action items.

☐ Using the book, *A Series of Unsuspecting Children's Poems*, write my **Values and Pillars List** and store it in my labeled TLC Save Forever Box(es) and/or TLC Journal/Binder(s). Use this list for action items and to have meaningful conversations with loved ones.

☐ Using the book, *How to Create a Financial Worksheet*, write my **Financial Nuts and Bolts List** and store it in my labeled TLC Save Forever Box(es) and/or TLC Journal/Binder(s). Use this list for action items and to inform key people of important information.

☐ Using the book, *When the Sun Goes Down: How to Enjoy the Night*, write my **Cozy and Comforting Nights List** and store it in my labeled TLC Save Forever Box(es) and/or TLC Journal/Binder(s). Use this list as action items to create cords of comfort and memories that strengthen relationships.

☐ Using the book, *Earth Adventures For Kids Fitness*, write my **Health and Wellness List** and store it in my labeled TLC Save Forever Box(es) and/or TLC Journal/Binder(s). Use this list for action items to improve life and inform others of helpful information.

☐ Be sure all TLC containers and Journal/Binder(s) are labeled with TLC labels for easy identification.

☐ Inform others that I have completed my TLC and let them know where it is stored.

☐ Join the Earth Adventures For Kids email list to be notified of updates, how-to videos, and special events and offers.

☐ Invite others to join me on different TLC activities and projects as I live the TLC life! I can document the memories with photos, mementos, and/or a quick write-up, and place the items into my TLC containers and/or Journal Binder(s).

☐ Go solo on some or all of my TLC and join the Earth Adventures For Kids email list for shared experiences of others who are going solo.

☐ How can the TLC Method be applied? For this space or situation, what is the mindset? What are the tools used? What are the systems in place? What are the products and services from the marketplace that can improve the space or situation?

OUR COACHING PROGRAMS:

Often, success is greater if we have help from those who have done what we want to do. Having an experienced coach walk us through the steps and create a dashboard of key points we need to monitor and be aware of when we have goals that we want to reach can help us keep on track through the start, the messy middle, and through the finish line. Coaching is a catalyst that helps get us where we want to go.

90-day Coaching Programs help you get where you want to go and are available in conjunction with the following Earth Adventures For Kids books:

1. *How to Create Your Own Signature Collection*

2. *How to Create a Treasure Legacy Collection*

3. *How to Create a Financial Worksheet*

Visit us at ForParents.EarthAdventuresForKids.com and scroll down to read about our coaching programs if you, or someone you know, would like help creating and implementing the following:

★ A Signature Collection

★ A Treasure Legacy Collection for you, for someone else, or in a loved one's memory

★ A Financial Worksheet

In addition, we also have coaching programs to help you:

★ **Create your 5 TLC Legacy Lists** generated from our books. Your TLC Legacy Lists can be used to develop your stories.

★ **Tell your stories** and get them into easy-to-access, enjoyable formats.

Gift our books, products, and coaching to others, as well as purchase them for your own use.

Take each of our quizzes to clarify how you are doing in the organization of home and office, finances, legacy, relationships, health and wellness, and overall quality of life. This is for your informational purposes only and will help you determine what areas you need to improve in and if coaching could help you achieve your goals faster and easier.

We have ways to help you write your stories. Go to ForParents.EarthAdventuresForKids.com and www.EarthAdventuresForKids.com to learn more about:

★ Low-cost monthly subscription service to help you Tell Your Stories, and complete your TLC and 5 TLC Legacy Lists.

★ One-on-one 90-day Coaching Programs to help you write your TLC Legacy Lists and your stories.

★ Webinar group coaching.

On our websites, go to the coaching section to learn more about how we can help you stay focused, move through the process in a manageable way, get your 5 TLC Legacy Lists written, your stories written, and get your TLC done and incorporated into your daily lifestyle with ease.

Our 90-day Coaching Program for
HOW TO CREATE YOUR OWN SIGNATURE COLLECTION

Identify areas where you need help, such as the organization of your home and office, finances, or improvement of legacy. We help you develop a plan and take the next steps to get where you want to go. We are simply the sounding board and a motivator, keeping you on track, and helping you get your tools and systems in place. Shopping The Marketplace for solutions helps you as well.

We use the book *How to Create Your Own Signature Collection* as a guide and have a weekly ninety-minute Zoom call. We will send you a coaching session form each week to complete before the Zoom call, and each week, you will have assigned tasks to do as you become familiar with the tools, systems, and The Marketplace using them to reach your goals.

Download our quiz at ForParents.EarthAdventureForKids.com or see the quiz section included in this book.

Our 90-day Coaching Program for
HOW TO CREATE A TREASURE LEGACY COLLECTION

Walk through the tasks of creating a Treasure Legacy Collection with us. We use the book *How to Create a Treasure Legacy Collection* as a guide and have a weekly ninety-minute Zoom call. We will send you a coaching session form each week to complete before the Zoom call, and each week, you will have assigned tasks to do as you progress through the stages of creating a Treasure Legacy Collection.

Download our quiz at ForParents.EarthAdventuresForKids.com or see the quiz section included in this book.

Our 90-day Coaching Program for
HOW TO CREATE A FINANCIAL WORKSHEET

Explore the tasks of creating a Financial Worksheet for you or a loved one with us and get used to using your Financial Worksheet regularly. We use the book *How to Create a Financial Worksheet* as a guide and have a weekly ninety-minute Zoom call. We will send you a coaching session form each week to complete before the Zoom call, and each week, you will have assigned tasks to do as you progress through the stages of creating a Financial Worksheet.

Download our quiz at ForParents.EarthAdventureForKids.com or see the quiz section included in this book.

Our 90-day Coaching Program for

CREATING YOUR 5 TLC LEGACY LISTS

Your TLC—tender, loving, care and Treasure Legacy Collection Lists are generated from our books. Read each of our books and write the following TLC Legacy Lists: *Activities in My Name List, Values and Pillars List, Financial Nuts and Bolts List, Cozy and Comforting Nights List, and Health and Wellness List*. Your TLC Legacy Lists can be used to write your stories. Our **TLC Legacy List 90-day Coaching Program** uses our books as a guide and we have a weekly 90-minute Zoom call. We send you a coaching session form each week to complete before our Zoom call and each week, you will have assigned tasks to do as you progress through the stages of creating your TLC Legacy Lists.

Our 90-day Coaching Program for

TELLING YOUR STORIES

Your stories preserved, in easy-to-access and enjoyable formats for you and others to enjoy is a way to help process and move through letting go of some of the physical items in your "stuff and piles." The value of preserving your stories as part of your Treasure Legacy Collection is priceless. Our **Telling Your Stories 90-day Coaching Program** uses our books and your TLC Legacy Lists as our guide. We have proven methods and formats, and we will help you progress through the stages of telling your stories. We will send you a coaching session form each week for you to complete with assigned tasks, before our 90-minute weekly Zoom call. You must create your TLC Legacy Lists prior to enrolling in this coaching program.

Our monthly subscription Coaching Program for

CREATING AND USING OUR LEGACY LIFESTYLE TLC METHOD

Subscribe to our low-cost monthly subscription to receive weekly reminders, assigned tasks, and other tips for keeping you on track with your Legacy Lifestyle and TLC Method to help you get organized in your home, office, and finances—improving relationships, health, and quality of life. Practice applying the TLC Method of Mindset, Tools, Systems, and Marketplace in situations and spaces.

OUR WEBINAR GROUP COACHING PROGRAM

Join our email list at www.EarthAdventuresForKids.com to get notified of our group coaching webinars that will focus on different parts of creating your TLC and living your legacy. These webinars promise to be powerful as our community can connect and share resources and ways that we are each making our TLC a way of life.

THE EARTH ADVENTURES FOR KIDS CERTIFIED LIFESTYLE COACH PROGRAMS

In addition to our coaching programs listed above, at certain times, we may take applications for our Earth Adventures For Kids Certified Lifestyle Coaching program that allows approved candidates to follow the Earth Adventures For Kids guidelines for establishing their own coaching business using the Earth Adventures For Kids books, tools, systems, and marketplace.

Earth Adventures For Kids Lifestyle Coaches have income-earning potential, with legitimate business tax deductions through their own independent contractor business. You can create an independently owned business with the potential for profit and/or loss.

All candidates and applicants must have read all the books by Earth Adventures For Kids, and must currently use the tools in established systems, having personal experience and success using our books and tools. Not all applicants will be approved, and we will only accept applications at certain times.

Our coaching programs are operated and managed by My Business Basics Coach, and you can learn more here: www.MyBusinessBasicsCoach/FreeGuide.com

The Earth Adventures For Kids TLC Method of Mindset, Tools, Systems, and Marketplace are all designed to help improve the following:

★ Organization in home and office

★ Organization in finances

★ Legacy

★ Relationships

★ Health and wellness

★ Quality of life

We look forward to hearing your success stories. Send them to us at Hello@EarthAdventuresForKids.com. Join our email list at www.EarthAdventuresForKids.com and be part of our community.

WORKSHEET AND GUIDE

**Use the following information as your own worksheet
to "do it yourself" and use our books as your guide.**

★ With each of our one-on-one 90-day Coaching Programs, we assist you with the following so that the entire process is more manageable and enjoyable.

★ Subscribe to our low-cost monthly service to keep you on track with creating your TLC, your Legacy Lifestyle, your 5 TLC Legacy Lists, and using the TLC Method.

★ We will also host webinars for low-cost group coaching, so be sure to join our email list to get notified of these opportunities.

YOUR GUIDE TO EXPERIENCE "TRANSFORMATION THROUGH ORGANIZATION"

Goal: To help you or another person(s) experience transformation through organization in a selected space. Use the following information as your own worksheet to move through the stages of organizing specific spaces. Use our books and this worksheet as your guide.

Our collections are collections of tools that help you get organized, improve your life and legacy, and live your best life now. Our two foundational books explain our two collections and how everything integrates.

1. Read *How to Create Your Own Signature Collection.*

2. Read *How to Create a Treasure Legacy Collection.*

After you read our books, you can use this worksheet to help you in the organization process. Some jobs are bigger than others, and some will have more people and tasks involved than others, so when you go through this comprehensive worksheet, some points may not apply to your situation.

Use this worksheet for the Earth Adventures For Kids process of creating:

★ Your Own Signature Collection

★ A Treasure Legacy Collection (TLC)

★ A Financial Worksheet

Whether you are creating your own Signature Collection, a Treasure Legacy Collection, or a Financial Worksheet, you will want to consider the following points in terms of whatever organizing process you are beginning. Each situation is unique, and every person is at a different stage in life with varying ranges of abilities and capacities to do more or less in certain spaces and areas.

USING THE TLC METHOD, WE DEVELOPED AND MAINTAINED:

★ our own signature lifestyle.

★ our TLC as a way of life.

★ our Financial Worksheet as a daily practice.

And you can do this too!

Ideally, we went through life in an organized way that helped us achieve our goals. We did have times of disequilibrium, chaos, unexpected challenges, and emergencies which we talk about in our books and in our Journal Stories on our Journal page at www.EarthAdventuresForKids.com. In our Journal Stories, we talk about how using our tools helped us get back into balance and move forward in life.

The idea is to start today with the process of transforming your life through organization and then building in the ways to maintain it through managing incoming, outgoing, and storage of items for a specific space. The information below is comprehensive and may or may not apply to your situation at this time. Keep in mind that the points below can be applied to creating your Signature Collection, your Treasure Legacy Collection, and creating your Financial Worksheet. With all that being said, let's get started!

Throughout this worksheet and guide, ask yourself,
"How can the TLC Method of Mindset, Tools, Systems, and Marketplace be applied?"

PLAN THE STRATEGY.

★ **Write down the whys.** Why do you need a change? What are the benefits?

★ Write down how life will be better for all involved when the job is done. What are the benefits? What if you do NOT take action—what will life continue to be like?

★ Acknowledge where you have been in the past in terms of this space, and then move forward. Many people have a space where they say, "Don't open that!" Meaning they have a lot of "stuff and piles" there and treasures hidden in their "stuff and piles" or some event that they may not want to deal with in that area. Be prepared for that reaction and discuss techniques for moving through past experiences in the space.

★ Make a list of the spaces that need improving and the benefits of improving those areas, proving that it is worth your time and effort to do it. Spaces include places such as rooms, closets, bathrooms, cars, finances, drawers, files, the garage, office, kitchen, and so forth.

★ Assess the present status quo in each space to be organized. Now and in the future—how do you handle incoming items, outgoing items, and storage for items in this space?

★ **Create the vision you want for your new spaces** and your new mode of operation—you, but better!

★ Understand the journey in the past and what the person(s) involved have been through.

★ What is the current status/present situation of the person(s) involved?

★ Where does the person(s) want to be in terms of how future life can look, ideally?

★ What has been done so far? What tasks still need to be completed?

★ What does each person involved need to understand in order to develop a plan of action?

★ What decisions do key person(s) need to make?

★ What steps do key person(s) need to take to get them through the beginning, middle, and end of the organization process?

★ Pre-determine what you will do if or when there is a point of the person(s) feeling like, "I need to be carried over the finish line!" Meaning, they are overwhelmed, tired, triggered, et cetera, and need extra support to finish the job.

★ It might help to have third-party professionals assist you in moving through the processes and spaces. Sometimes, it is easier to refer sensitive topics to others who are not as attached. Our team can help guide you through. Assess if professional counseling is needed, including advisors in legal, tax, financial, and mental health, and wellness.

CHECKLISTS HELP YOU KEEP ON TRACK.

★ **Print our checklists, bullet point lists, and worksheets from this book** and put them on a clipboard for easy reference, to take notes on, and to track your progress as you complete tasks.

★ **Use our checklists and create your own checklists** with ours to plan the work. Include information on completed sections of work tasks to be done with the details on who, what, when, how, where, and why.

★ **Send your checklists** to those involved in that section of the work. This way, everyone is on the same page and understands the next steps, their involvement, and the strategy.

WRITE AND USE YOUR 5 TLC LEGACY LISTS.

★ *How to Create a Treasure Legacy Collection* shows the power of writing your 5 TLC Legacy Lists and how they build your legacy, improve your relationships and quality of life, and help bridge the gap between heaven and earth.

★ *How to Create Your Own Signature Collection* shows the power of using your 5 TLC Legacy Lists in decision-making as they help define your classic, your goals, and your priorities so you can make decisions aligned with the results you want to get.

★ **Our coaching programs can help you write your lists for your Treasure Legacy Collection.** Need help writing out your 5 TLC Legacy Lists? Get our assistance. Over the course of ninety days, we will help you complete your lists for the following: 1) Activities in My Name List, 2) Values and Pillars List, 3) Financial Nuts and Bolts List, 4) Cozy and Comforting Nights List, and 5) Health and Wellness List. You must have read the corresponding books before signing up for the TLC Legacy List coaching program.

DECISION-MAKING; KEEP MOVING FORWARD.

★ It might help to have third-party professionals assist you in moving through the processes. Sometimes it is easier to refer sensitive topics to others who are not as attached. Our team can help guide you through. Assess if professional counseling is needed, including legal, tax, financial, and mental health and wellness.

★ **Use your 5 TLC Legacy Lists as your guide**. They will help you make decisions and keep moving forward when you get organized, and they will help you develop your Signature Lifestyle, and live your Legacy Lifestyle. Choices made can depend on what you have on your

5 TLC Legacy Lists. Use the 5 TLC Legacy Lists as your decision-making criterion so you stay true to your goals, values, and priorities, and stay true to your authentic self.

★ **Have a pre-determined plan to help get all involved through the "sorting and deciding of the stuff and piles" phase**. Decide to power through with quick decisions—all the way through to the very last item in the space. If it helps, you can make this a mantra and repeat it to each other: "Power through the sorting-and-deciding-of-the-stuff-and-piles-phase to the very last item in this space." And say it with a big smile! All things are becoming new! Be excited for the new creation in your space(s).

★ You can decide to use a "clean slate batching technique" to clear a space quickly.

★ Section the work into manageable stages. Assign tasks with details of who, what, when, how, where, and why. Ask friends and family to join in or decline certain sections of the process. Memories are made here. Make it fun with food, drinks, breaks, and walks down memory lane. Hire out certain tasks to add in extra support.

★ **Coming to terms with it all**. Whatever the past has been, whatever events have occurred, whatever the triggers are, and whatever the highs and lows have been, we choose to recognize divine interventions and divine purpose as a way for us to come to terms with it all—the good, the bad, the ugly. This can be whatever works for you, but for us, we see an element of the divine at work, and we turn our ashes into beauty, like nutrients for new growth.

★ **Remember, we ALL have "stuff and piles" to deal with**. You are not alone. Find the human experience in this process, and as best you can, move through it with grace and enjoy it. There is a personal responsibility element to this endeavor, especially if your "stuff and piles" are affecting or will affect others.

★ Use The Megaphone for fun and effective communication during the "sorting and deciding through all the stuff and piles" phase.

TIPS FOR LETTING GO OF STUFF.

★ **Write your stories for your Treasure Legacy Collection,** which helps extract meaning and value—worthiness—from all the items you will be sorting, making decisions on, and choosing how to handle in terms of deciding to keep, toss, repurpose, donate, gift, or sell.

★ Story writing can include taking pictures of physical items and attaching the story to them. We have found this makes it easier to let the item go to donate it, gift it, or sell it, and get it out of your physical space for others to enjoy. A digital reminder is nice in the form of pictures and stories about the item(s).

★ **If you are gifting, consider the recipient and their ability to accommodate item(s)**. Sometimes the gifting can just be the digital photo, video, or collage reminder of the physical item to make the "treasure" compact, easy to store, and easy to protect—because it is in a digital format, and it is not the actual physical item!

★ **If you have social media accounts, you can post sentimental, meaningful pictures or videos**. For generations to come, they will be able to access these accounts and posts.

As always, be mindful of others, including safety and security, and be wise in your posts. For the first time in history, people can go to their loved one's accounts for memories and information, so those who are creating accounts and posts now will have created history for future generations—imagine future generations learning about their ancestry through their relative's social media posts!

★ Creating digital reminders of physical items with your best stories about them and making your 5 TLC Legacy Lists will make it easier to part with the physical items. Getting the stories and photos attached together and into easy-to-access and enjoyable formats helps you move through letting go of items.

★ We have found these practices to be invaluable in helping others to move through their "stuff and piles" and spaces with confirmation that their life is appreciated and has meaning, value, and purpose. It helps them to see that they are preserving the history, the memories, and sharing the knowledge with others to help others enjoy the items and receive the lessons learned, the value, and "carry the torch" into the next generations.

★ **Coming to terms with the "good money paid" for certain items** or the bargains enjoyed when getting the items or the history of the item or the other stories and attachments involved, is a process that can be practiced. Acknowledge the money involved, the time, the memories, the value, and the history with your 5 TLC Legacy Lists and by telling your stories in enjoyable formats we discuss in our TLC book.

★ As you go through your "stuff and piles" you are processing your past, choosing to keep the best, and creating your new future, moving forward into your best life now.

★ **You can make donations of items and their attached stories in the name of certain people as a way of celebrating and honoring the people, the memories, the history, and the value.** Consider reaching out to museums, foundations, charities, businesses, designers, organizers, video and photography professionals, media, social media, churches, and so forth to find people who can help receive and document the items and the stories. We can help facilitate this process if you like. Email us at Hello@EarthAdventuresForKids.com and we will send your requests to our wide community and networks to help match you with possibilities if we can.

★ Make sure trusted, loved ones you would like to give access to are informed of 1) how to access and 2) how to use your TLC in your absence, no matter what phase of creating your TLC you are in.

TIPS TO GET THROUGH THE BEGINNING, MIDDLE, AND END OF THE WORK:

★ **Work Focus Zones** can be scheduled in blocks of ninety minutes, where you do deep work and really move through the task at hand. Have dedicated work time in blocks of thirty, sixty, or ninety minutes with brief breaks in between if needed. Set an alarm and choose to keep working if you are "in the zone."

★ Have custom **music playlists ready to go** for each type of work. I like Hawaiian music as it relaxes me. I also enjoy reggae, and sometimes, if I really need to go all out, maybe even some "rocker" music. Whatever speaks to you and allows the work to flow and be productive. Some like classical, some like 80's, and my dad enjoys 50's music. Tap into your inspiration and motivation music to help you make it through.

★ **Decide who will do what.** Add in extra support when needed. Volunteers, charities, friends and family, and paid services like Thumbtack and TaskRabbit can help, including professional cleaning companies. Make sure people are vetted and from a trusted source you are comfortable with. Some help may need to come from other professionals such as counselors, tax and legal advisors, financial advisors, accountants, and so forth.

★ **Take before, during, and after photos** and document your "transformation through organization" success stories using the TLC Method.

★ **If this project is a large job, with many people involved and in different locations**, you can consider some of those involved attending the TLC sessions virtually through Zoom or a different virtual platform. Also, consider that some may want to donate funds to complete the tasks with others on-site physically and others may attend virtually. You have many hybrid options today with a range of flexibility thanks to technology!

★ **Virtual organizing works!** You, or another person, can pay a professional moving or organizing company to be on-site while you, and/or others attend the TLC cleaning session virtually. In-person is best in many cases due to the "creating memories and strengthening bonds" factor, but some sections of the work stages can be completed virtually with trusted and vetted paid professionals or volunteers. We offer virtual organizing services through Zoom, just go to our coaching section to learn more. You can email us with any direct questions and join our email list to get notified of our new releases, events, and special offers.

★ **Decide to dedicate a day, a weekend, or a week** here and there over a month, a quarter, or a year. Friends and family can choose what days and times work for them. Let friends and family help plan the food, drinks, and music so everyone enjoys the time as best they can. Sandwich platters, large salads to go, an ice chest of cold drinks, and maybe an evening dinner out will help motivate the troops.

★ **Make the process as enjoyable as possible** and use the time to create wonderful moments and the path to your new future in new spaces! Creating your Signature Collection, Treasure Legacy Collection, and Financial Worksheet in a non-hurried, non-emergency way that is planned and enjoyed with loved ones is a better way to go than leaving it for a time when it must be dealt with in crisis mode. At some point, we all have to deal with our "stuff and piles."

★ **Sometimes, it is easier to "clean slate" a space and haul everything out for off-site sorting and decision-making.** Then, only bring back the "best of the best" and the most needed items. The rest of the items, or the "stuff and piles," can go on a trailer or a U-Haul to donate the items to a trusted person, organization, or business so they can do the sorting and deciding, determining what can be re-used, re-purposed, re-cycled, and donated to the best place. You can delegate the decision-making to someone else if there is a lot of "stuff and piles," and they can do this process off-site so you can begin to enjoy creating your new spaces. Remember, you can take pictures of the items, tell your stories integrated with the pictures, and get everything into an enjoyable format.

AS PART OF YOUR SIGNATURE LIFESTYLE AND LEGACY LIFESTYLE, YOU COULD REACH OUT TO HELP OTHERS.

★ **Consider helping your loved ones** complete their "transformation through organization," and helping them develop their own Signature Lifestyle, create their Treasure Legacy Collection, or Financial Worksheet as a way of volunteering your time. Many people do not have the assistance needed to complete these important organizational strategies that yield great benefits.

★ If you belong to an organization or business, consider that many people do not have loved ones to help them create their Treasure Legacy Collection. As an organization or business, you could donate time, supplies, money, and so forth to help people complete their Treasure Legacy Collection as a charity and act of goodwill. Always use vetted and trusted organizations and businesses for safety and security reasons.

★ The above is the same for the Signature Collection and Signature Lifestyle. If you know of someone who could benefit from a "transformation through organization" experience, you could work with an organization or business to help others or donate your time on your own to help others with their "stuff and piles."

★ If you love helping others, consider becoming a Certified Earth Adventures For Kids Lifestyle Coach as an independent contractor with your own business with profit and loss potential, including the potential for business tax deductions.

USE OUR BOOKS IN DIFFERENT WAYS.

★ Our other books each play important parts in the comprehensive picture of improving your life and legacy and living your best life now; this is discussed in each book, so be sure to read all our books.

★ You will find new applications and meanings as you get familiar with the books and tools, creating and developing your own systems with them. So be sure to buy all our books and get all the tools for a complete collection.

★ Give our books as gifts to others and you can discuss the concepts, ideas, practices, habits, and tools.

SHARE OUR LINKS WITH YOUR FRIENDS AND FAMILY

so they can opt-in to join our email list and get updates on events, special offers, and new releases. Visit us at ForParents.EarthAdventuresForKids.com and www.EarthAdventuresForKids.com for all our books and tools to help with your journey on the road to success.

THANK YOU FOR READING
OUR COMPREHENSIVE, ULTIMATE GUIDE.

We have done our best to make this error-free. If you find an error, send us an email and we will fix it in the next edition! This is my way of letting go and moving on to the next step, knowing I have done my best, but we are all imperfect, and that is OK!

The Earth Adventures For Kids TLC Method of Mindset, Tools, Systems, and Marketplace is designed to help improve the following:

- ✓ Organization in home and office
- ✓ Organization in finances
- ✓ Legacy
- ✓ Relationships
- ✓ Health and wellness
- ✓ Quality of life

We look forward to hearing your success stories. Send them to us at:
Hello@EarthAdventuresForKids.com.

Join our email list at www.EarthAdventuresForKids.com and be part of our community.

BE OUR NEXT SUCCESS STORY.

**The information below will help you jumpstart your journey,
and get on the road to success with our roadmap!**

- ✓ Read our Journal Stories on our website Journal page at www.EarthAdventuresForKids.com as they tell how we used each tool and why we wrote each book.

- ✓ Our books and Journal Stories tell the ways we have used each tool and integrated them into systems to not only manage incoming items, outgoing items, and storage for various spaces but also to improve relationships and quality of life, helping us to reach our goals.

- ✓ Use the checklists and worksheets to help you get our tools, develop your systems, and experience the ultimate transformation through organization, using our TLC Method.

- ✓ Develop your own signature story of how the TLC Method has improved your life and legacy, and helps you live your best life .

ACKNOWLEDGMENTS

We thank all those who have helped on the journey of raising our kids and those who helped our parents who raised us! We thank not only the parents, but also the extended family, the varied teachers of all kinds, the caregivers, the administrators, the doctors, the healthcare professionals, the artists, the musicians, the creators, the doers, the dreamers, the spiritual guidance counselors, the divine, the writers, the builders, the activity directors and coaches, the employers, the co-workers, the community, and all who come into the patchwork quilting of life, and the circle of life. One moment and one day at a time, the needle and thread actions weave a unique quilt we can look at and say, "Hey, this turned out beautiful." Each of you played a part!

FROM THE

ORIGINAL

EARTH ADVENTURES FOR KIDS

Our books are the ultimate guides to improving your life and legacy, and living your best life now. We grew up the Earth Adventures For Kids way.

As young adults, we still use all the tools and books as guides for so much of our lives. Start reading our book series today. Learn more about us at www.EarthAdventuresForKids.com.

Ash

Andrea

Ani

Example of a photo collage created in Canva. You can do this with your photos too!

Made in the USA
Middletown, DE
16 March 2024

50982915R00071